the Covenant Coat

the Covenant Coat

A Novel of Joseph

Robert H. Moss

Distributed by:

Granite Publishing and Distribution, LLC
868 North 1430 West
Orem, Utah 84057
(801) 229-9023 • Toll Free (800) 574-5779
Fax (801) 229-1924

Cover painting used by permission of
The Church of Jesus Christ of Latter-day Saints

Robert H. Moss
9851 Petunia Way,
Sandy UT 84092
rmoss34@comcast.net
www.roberthmoss.com

ISBN-13: 978-1-56684-678-3
ISBN-10: 1-56684-678-1

Library of Congress Catalog Card Number:
2006937201

Printed 2006 in the United States of America
FC Printing, Salt Lake City, UT

About the Author

Robert Moss was born in the little town of Santa Clara, Utah, on 3 March 1934. All four sets of great-grandparents were Mormon pioneers who arrived in Utah prior to the railroad's coming in 1869.

After he completed high school, Robert married Roberta Renner. Before any children came along, Robert joined the Utah National Guard and served in the Guard for 31 years, the last eighteen years as a chaplain. He served as group chaplain with the 19th Special Forces Group, and was called the "jumping chaplain," being qualified as a senior parachutist and jumpmaster. During the Desert Storm War he was recalled to active duty and served as senior chaplain responsible for establishing and directing nine family assistance centers in the Utah area. His duties included working with all families who had family members serving overseas during the war. He established procedures for advisement and help in the areas of financial and legal assistance, and personal and family counseling.

He attended Dixie College and completed their two-year program, graduating with an Associate of Science degree. Their first son, Steven Robert, was born soon after his graduation. In January of 1955, Robert volunteered for active duty in the army, and after basic training was sent to Germany. Roberta joined him overseas and they were able to travel extensively throughout Europe.

Upon completion of his military obligation he returned to school and finished his bachelor's degree at Utah State University in elementary education. By the time four years of college were completed, he and Roberta had four children, Steven, Kenneth, Alan, and Bryan. He taught school for four years while working on his Master's degree from Brigham Young University. With his master's degree in School Administration, he took his first administrative position as an elementary school principal in Wyoming. After serving as principal for a period of time, he accepted the position of Superintendent of Schools, also in Wyoming. Upon completion of his doctorate he became a professor of education at the University of Northern Colorado.

An offer came from Southern Utah State College, now Southern Utah University, to return to Utah to teach. Though it meant less money, home and family ties were strong. Robert brought his family back to Cedar City, Utah. Their fifth son, Dennis, was born while teaching at Southern Utah State College

From his youth Robert had a desire to write and had a large file of projects he wanted to complete. In 1975, he and Roberta started a part-time business in order to give him the necessary time to write and the income to support his family. Because of his business, Robert was able to “retire” from teaching in 1980. He has written nine books on the Book of Mormon. Eight of them are novels about his heroes of the Book of Mormon. He named the series The Nephite Chronicles. He has also written a biography of his younger brother, who was a downs syndrome child, entitled Celestial Child, and a Moss Family History. He wrote an historical novel of the Utah War, Soldiers ’n Saints. His newest novel, Through Deepening Trials, was released in June. Currently he has five (5) books being published as ebooks: Sword of Kah, The Successful Entrepreneur, Slavery to Riches, The Prophets Speak: Education and Knowledge, and The Prophets Speak: The Constitution.

Married fifty-four (54) years, he and Roberta now live in Salt Lake City where he devotes his time to church, business, and writing.

Books by Robert H. Moss

The Nephite Chronicles
- *Covenant Coat:* A Novel of Joseph
- *I Nephi:* A Novel of Nephi and His Family
- *Waters of Mormon:* A Novel of Alma, The Elder
- *That I Were An Angel:* A Novel of Alma, The Younger
- *Title of Liberty:* A Novel of Moroni and Helaman
- *The Abridger:* A Novel of Mormon
- *Valiant Witness:* A Novel of Moroni
- *Capstone of Faith:* A Testimony of the Book of Mormon

Celestial Child: A Biography of a Downs-Syndrome Child
Through Deepening Trials
(A Historical Novel of the Martin Handcart Company)
The Moss Family: 1837-1993
Guts But No Glory (A Novel of the Utah War)
A Readers' Old Testament Digest
A Readers Book of Mormon Digest
Slavery to Riches
On Wings of Eagles: The Positive Christian PMA for LDS
The Mad King and the Musician
(A Historical Novel of King Ludwig and Wagner)

I dedicate this book
to my wife and helpmeet, Roberta.
With her servant heart and willingness to sacrifice,
she has been a Rachel to her family.

Contents

Preface

The story of Joseph continues to intrigue humanity. Rachel, his mother, died during the birth of her second son, Benjamin, when Joseph was eight years of age. Jacob, Joseph's father, adored Rachel. He worked more than fourteen years for the right to marry her. After her death he mourned her for the rest of his life.

Jacob was very protective of his youngest sons. He did not permit Joseph to have the obstacle-overcoming experiences his older brothers faced. As a child, Joseph was favored and spoiled. He remained close to his father's tent. Is it any wonder his brothers resented him? What changed in him? How did he develop the principles that turned him from the lowliest of slaves to the wealthiest of men? Perhaps God gave Joseph the opportunity to become more consecrated by taking everything from him. Many people, like Joseph, have sufficient faith to avoid committing sin, but not enough faith to sacrifice time in order to focus on one's omissions. Joseph's slavery put him a position to give total consecration — thus his unconditional surrender became a total victory in time.

Each man and woman, regardless of what age he or she lives in, can be a slave — a slave to thoughts, a slave to habit, a slave to the economic system, a slave to a dead-end job, a slave to addictive substances. How does one overcome slavery? How does one overcome slave mentality? The lessons of Joseph can put us in a position to be a doer, an overcomer, an achiever.

Joseph set an example for those who believe lives can change. He made dramatic changes in his own life, leaving the spoiled child image behind to become a leader of his people and heir of the covenant God made with his great-grandfather, Abraham. He changed: from taking to giving; from dependency to independence; from arrogance to humility; from following to great leadership; from slave to king.

Perhaps his strongest trait was his servant heart. George Elliot once asked, "What do we live for, if not to make life less difficult for others?" Through hardships and adversity, Joseph learned to become a servant in every situation in which he found himself. Through serving, he became a leader, prospering in all circumstances. He found that the law of the harvest always works: whatsoever we give comes back manyfold. Joseph also exemplified the character trait of forgiveness. His brothers sold him as a slave. He spent many years as a slave or in prison, separated for over twenty years from those he loved. He had reason to hate and seek revenge. Instead, he forgave readily and repaid treachery with love.

Prologue

After God drove Adam and Eve from the Garden of Eden, they accepted the task of carving a new life from the land. "By the sweat of their brow" they digged, planted, reaped, and harvested. Soon their descendants covered the land, a prophetic lineage extending from Adam to Noah. Shem, Noah's son, carried on the blessing through his lineage. The seed of Shem passed through ten generations until the birth of Terah.

Terah, Abram's father, with the rest of his clan, lived for a time outside the walled city of Ur, a bustling, prosperous commercial center already old when Abram was born. Nomad blood flowed through the veins of Abram and his people. Wanderers all, they moved with their flocks. At home in the plains, meadows and hills, these Nomads hated Ur's narrow, crooked streets, which ran between windowless, unbaked-brick buildings. When grass disappeared in the valley of Ur, Abram and his clan made their way up the Euphrates Valley. Sarai, Abram's petite wife, rode a small reddish-brown donkey beside her husband. Lot, Abram's nephew, tended a mixed flock of goats and sheep nearby. Asses carried the tents. Servants and slaves carried water jars, provisions, and the few possessions needed by the nomadic wanderers.

Terah and his clan settled in Haran. Abram and his wife Sarai lived in a tent, pastured their flocks in Padanaram, and prospered. Abram's father, Terah, however, returned to the practice of idolatry. Abram, a righteous and God-fearing man, went into the hills above Haran and prayed mightily to the Lord. The Lord appeared to him, saying, "Arise and take Lot with thee, for I have purposed to take thee away out of Haran, and to make of thee a minister to bear my name in a strange land which I will give unto thy seed for an everlasting possession, when they hearken to my voice."

Under the Lord's guidance, Abram led his clan southward in spring when pastures ahead still glowed green from winter rains. On a bright sunshiny summer day they crossed the Jordan River and entered the land of Canaan — the land God had promised them. After pitching his tent in Shechem, Abram built an altar to worship the one true God. Here he received the Covenant — a binding promise from God. Here he also met Noah's aged son, Shem. From him he received instruction in the worship of the One God.

When a famine devastated the Land of Canaan, Abram moved his tents again — this time to Egypt. Years later he moved back to the promised land where his dream of an heir was finally realized with the birth of Isaac. The Lord changed Abram's name to Abraham — "the father is exalted." Sarai became Sarah — "princess of the Lord." Eventually each of their sons, Ishmael and Isaac, became fathers of nations.

Isaac married Rebekah and carried the patriarchal line and God's covenant through his two sons, Esau and Jacob. Jacob, the second son, gained the birthright through his mother's deception, then fled to Haran to escape Esau's wrath. While there, he sought a wife from his relative's family. After serving his mother's brother, Laban, for more than fourteen years, the beautiful Rachel was finally his.

Years later, with several wives and concubines and eleven stalwart sons, he returned with his tents to the land of his covenanted inheritance. Joseph, his youngest at that time, was his favorite.

Chapter 1: In the Pit

Scratching and clawing for a handhold, Joseph jumped once more against the steep side of the pit, again falling helplessly to the floor. He looked at his fingers, scraped and bleeding from many desperate attempts to climb out of the bottle-shaped well. He sat there, discouraged, on the dank floor. He could see no possible way to climb out of the hole into which his brothers had put him.

He was hoarse, his throat raw from yelling. He stood, cupped his hands, and shouted once again. "My brothers, what have I done to you? How have I sinned? Am I not of your bones and flesh? Is not Jacob your father, my father? Why do you do this thing to me?"

No response. He looked up at the night sky, seeing only a circle of stars. A terrifying loneliness overcame him. The hole seemed so dark and so quiet! He shivered, more from fear than from the cold. Sitting down again he drew his knees to his chin, discouraged and disconsolate, hungry, thirsty, and cold. Except for his loincloth, he was naked. The well was cold and damp. He wished he had his long-sleeved coat. The dark dismal hours passed slowly. In his exhaustion, he finally slept.

He woke, stretched his arms and looked around. A circle of light above told him pale dawn had finally come, though no sunlight penetrated the muskiness of the pit. A slight sound caught his attention. A large scorpion, wicked tail curved menacingly over its back, scampered from a hole. Joseph screamed and jumped to his feet. Picking up a broken stone he ground the scorpion to a pulp. The bottom of the well remained in deep shadow. Were there serpents also? Shivering again, he pressed his thin body tightly against the wall.

He called loudly, "Judah! Simeon! Levi! My brethren, please lift me out of this place of darkness." He listened. No response. He shouted again. "Have compassion on me, your younger brother. If I have sinned against you, I am sorry. Surely you will pull me out for our father's sake." Silence again greeted his cries. Again he tried yelling, but his voice had fled in defeat. He clutched at his throat and looked fearfully into the dark pit. Tears of frustration and self-pity welled in his eyes and overflowed down his dirty cheeks. He wept unashamedly.

After several tear-filled moments, he straightened his shoulders. With the back of his hands he resolutely wiped away the tears. Standing there, he prayed aloud, "God of Abraham, I need your help. You gave me the power to dream and to interpret dreams. Now give me power to remove myself from this place."

He waited, hoping for some miracle. Nothing happened. He looked around dejected. The pit isolated him from the living — buried him in the earth. Even God had stopped listening. He wrapped his arms around his body, squeezing what warmth he could into his bare skin. Then he spoke aloud again, getting some comfort from his own voice. "O, that my father knew what my brothers have done to me. He would take care of them." Just saying it made him feel better.

He looked up again at the circle of blue sky above him. The top of the well lay about fifteen feet above his head, but it might as well have been a hundred. "El Shaddai, God of Abraham, you have taught our people that we are your children — that you are our Father In Heaven. Protect me from the scorpions and the serpents. Rescue me from this place." Wearily he again sat down. Cold and hunger numbed his senses. If he stayed in the pit, he would surely starve, unless scorpions and serpents got him first. As he sat, he had time to pursue his thoughts.

* * *

Months before, his father's vast flocks had grazed the hills of Hebron to ground level. Joseph's older brothers had taken the flocks north to feed on the grassy hillsides near Shechem.

"Joseph," Jacob called.

Joseph moseyed into his father's tent. "What is it, Father. You interrupted my studies."

A lightly bearded youth of seventeen, Joseph stood tall and straight before his father. He saw the pride in Jacob's eyes. He knew he looked imposing in his short, brown wool skirt hemmed with red. He also wore a broad leather belt decorated with copper rivets. Bronze hilts of his copper sword and dagger protruded from his belt. A leather band laced with gold wire circled his forehead, holding his long brown hair in place.

"Son, your brothers pasture the flocks in Shechem. They should have returned home by now. Please go see what keeps them."

Joseph had not been anxious to leave the comforts of Mamre to travel the sixty miles on foot to Shechem. Obediently, though, he mentally prepared himself for the journey. The trip was distasteful to him. He knew his brothers disliked him. What kind of reception would they would give him? "Take a full skin of water with you. Your aunt Bilhah will bake bread for your journey. Four or five loaves should be sufficient. Date palms and fig trees grow along the way." Jacob put a loving hand on Joseph's shoulder. "Be careful. Many dangers wait between here and Shechem. Don't travel after dark. There are predatory lions and wolves, and even wild dogs along the way. Stop and build a fire before the sun sets." He added, "You will pass through the land of the Amorites. They are a warlike and dangerous people."

Joseph kissed his father goodbye and went to find Bilhah. She stood by the oven, kneading barley flour and water into bread dough. With supple fingers she stirred in some honey. When the dough was thoroughly mixed, she formed perfect rounds and dropped them onto the upturned clay platters. Joseph loved raisins and Bilhah carefully spotted some of the rounds with the sweet dried fruit. She placed the platters in the hot beehive oven for baking. While the bread cooked, Joseph went to say goodbye to Benjamin.

A cheerful youth, nine-year-old Benjamin played in the sand outside Jacob's tent. Joseph sneaked up behind him and pinned his arms to his sides. Benjamin cried out in fear, then realizing who had pinned him, struggled valiantly against the arms that held him. He finally went limp and turned his head to Joseph with a broad smile. Joseph released him and sat on the sand beside him.

"Look at my rocks." Benjamin held out a handful of smooth stones. "I found them on the hill."

Joseph handled the stones, rounded by centuries of erosion. "They are very pretty," he said.

Benjamin looked at him. "Father said he sends you to Shechem. Can I go?"

Joseph laughed. "That would be fun, little brother, but much too dangerous. Didn't father tell you about the lions and robbers?"

"I still want to go,"

Joseph shook his head. "No, I must travel quickly. I will be back within the week. Then perhaps we can hike together."

Benjamin picked out a greenish-colored agate and thrust it at Joseph. "Here. Take my prettiest rock."

Smiling broadly, Joseph accepted Benjamin's gift. "Thank you. I shall keep it always with me." He slipped the stone into his waistband and promptly forgot about it. From his leather belt he took a small dagger. "Here is my present to you." Benjamin's eyes shone as he accepted the dagger.

When Joseph returned to Bilhah's tent, the bread was ready, slightly burned on the bottom and crisp on top. Joseph placed it in his pack without so much as a "thank you" to Bilhah.

The trail from Mamre to Shechem was clearly defined, marked by watershed on one side and deep valleys on the other. Where the path skirted steep hillsides with their many boulders and scraggly bushes, Joseph exercised great caution. Such hillsides would be excellent hiding places for robbers. Not wanting to take any chances, he gave them as wide a berth as possible.

He hoped to find his brothers quickly so he could return home to his father's tent. He had to admit that, compared to those out with the flocks, he had an easy life. While he enjoyed Mamre's comforts, his brothers endured the heat of the day and the cold of the night, along with a monotonous diet of goat's milk, olives, raisins, and goat cheese.

The sun stood at its high point by the time Joseph reached Ephrath. This place had much meaning for him. Ephrath, called Bethlehem by some, was a sacred spot to him. Here his mother lay buried. He found her grave and knelt, memories of his youth vivid in his mind.

The family had camped here while on their way to Hebron to dwell with his grandfather, Isaac. His mother, heavy with child, had started her labor while camped at this spot. Joseph, eight, played in the sand under one of the large terebinth trees while his half-brothers set up the goat-hair tent. He remembered his mother's piercing screams. Elkah, one of her maids, rushed out of the tent. Jacob, agonizing nearby, stepped forward, an anxious look on his face. The maid raised her hands high in the air, then prostrated herself before Jacob. He gently pulled her to her feet. Joseph had not been close enough to hear what she said, but he saw his father's look of anguish.

Jacob looked around. "Joseph, your mother wants to see you."

Hand in hand, he and his father entered the tent. His mother lay on the floor on a pile of rugs. Her face, usually full of life, was white as goat's milk. Her eyes shone dully without their usual joyful luster. She weakly held out her arm to Joseph, pulling him close, then held him there, while she whispered softly into his ear. He had been surprised at the wetness of her hair. After her hug, he pulled away and started back out to play. Another scream rose to a wailing crescendo, then abruptly stopped. He turned, not knowing what to do. One of the maids gently pushed him out into the bright sunlight. His father came slowly from the tent, his head hanging almost on his chest. Leah, his mother's sister, followed closely, a tiny bundle in her arms.

She caught up with him. "Jacob, you have another son," she said softly. "But why? Why did she have to die?" Jacob's voice broke as he angrily shouted. His hands clenched into fists as he raised his arms to the heavens. He turned away from Leah, apparently not wishing her to see the tears of grief coursing down his brown cheeks.

Joseph had never seen a face so filled with sorrow. The pain of his father cut through him like a sword. He hid behind a bush — trying to separate himself from the agony he saw. His mother dead? He had seen animals die. He knew what death meant. But his Mother? Feeling a loss he did not understand, he ran to his father, throwing his arms around Jacob's legs.

Leah stepped beside Jacob. "Rachel took pride in bringing you another son. But I think she knew she was going to die." She walked around to face him, then looked at Jacob, almost accusingly. "Jacob, Rachel was almost fifty years old. In her frail condition she was too old to have another baby." She paused as the baby in the blanket whimpered, then she uncovered its tiny, wrinkled face for Jacob to see. "Before she died, she named the baby Benoni, son of my sorrow."

Jacob took the tiny bundle in his arms, rocking gently and crooning to the baby. He spoke as if to himself. "The boy shall be named Benjamin, the son of my right hand." He gave the baby back to Leah and took Joseph by the hand. Wearily, he sat on a nearby boulder, lifting young Joseph to his knee. "My son," he began, then choked, his face wrinkled in his sorrow. Regaining his composure, he continued. "My son, your mother left us and returned to the One God who gave her life. We have her no more." He bowed his head in anguish. Several times he tried to talk, but his voice choked. He breathed deeply, sighed, and said, "Joseph, your mother gave you a brother before she left us." He reached over, and with his hand tilted up Joseph's chin so he could look him in the eyes. "Promise me that you will always look after your younger brother. He will always be a reminder to us of your mother." Joseph nodded mutely.

"Aunt Bilhah will now be your mother." Jacob saw the hurt in Joseph's eyes. "She will care for you and Benjamin." He put Joseph down, turned, and stumbled off into the terebinth grove.

As he knelt now at his mother's grave, Joseph remembered how his father had moved his bed into Bilhah's tent to identify her as his new favorite. Reuben came back from herding sheep, learned what had happened, and stalked to Bilhah's tent. He dumped his father's bed outside in the sand, then, in great anger, went in search of his father. Joseph had been playing in the sand near his father when his oldest brother stalked up. "Why do you dishonor my mother, Leah?" Reuben stammered in his anger.

Redness of anger spread across Jacob's face, but Reuben continued. "All of us know that Rachel was your favorite wife. Now she is dead you again trample Leah, your first wife, in the sand of the desert by showing preference for a mere handmaid." Reuben's hands clenched at his sides. His face grew livid.

Jacob leaned back and studied his son's young, dark face, now contorted with anger. Smell of sheep permeated Reuben's clothes, but he had no humility in his manner. Breathing deeply to control his own anger, Jacob finally replied. "Reuben, you are my eldest son. The birthright should have been yours, but you have defiled your father's bed. I take the birthright from you and give it to Joseph, the eldest son of my second wife."

Young as he was, Joseph could see that his father's response totally shocked Reuben. He stood for several moments, as if rooted to the earth, before he turned and stumbled off in the direction of the flock. He had been so upset he had not returned to the camp for over a month. After Reuben's angry departure, Jacob called Joseph to his tent, laid his hands on his head, and pronounced a blessing upon him.

As he knelt at his mother's grave, Joseph attempted to recall the words of that blessing. Jacob had told him, "... the blessing of your great-grandfather, Abraham, and your grandfather, Isaac, will be yours. Through you their blessing will be realized. Your posterity will fill the earth." He promised Joseph that the Lord had a special mission for him that would be revealed at the appropriate time. His father then pronounced the patriarchal blessing upon him, granting the birthright, now rightfully his.

At thirteen, when he became a man, his father gave him a beautiful, white, long-sleeved woolen coat embroidered with many colors. The coat symbolized a token of his birthright, proof to him and his brothers that he remained the favored one of the family. He knew his brothers resented him, but he really did not care. The thought came to him, perhaps I have been a little haughty in my treatment of my brothers, but after all, the Lord showed me in dreams that I would someday rule over them.

He had not realized how long he knelt by his mother's grave. The last rays of the sun cast strange shadows around him and projected a flickering aura over the mountains. He shivered involuntarily as he looked around in the mysterious twilight. Remembering what his father had told him, he gathered wood for a large fire. He stockpiled extra wood so he could feed the fire during the night. At last he slept, curled up in his coat in the soft sand.

Shivering with the pre-dawn coolness, he awakened before the sun rose over the eastern hills. He resumed his journey, eating a meager breakfast of bread and dates while he walked. The countryside he passed through, the variegated green of lush vegetation, contrasted sharply with the drabness of desert around the oasis of Mamre where his family lived. White puffs of clouds spotted the bright blue sky above him. There seemed a strange stillness in the air, as if he alone walked the earth. When he came to a stream, he squatted beside it, splashing cool water on his hot face. He kicked off his sandals, soaking his feet in the stream's cool depths. Standing there, ankle-deep, he looked around at the land — a choice land — the land of his inheritance. Joseph joyed at being alive.

Shadows lengthened by the time he arrived at Shechem. The sun set over the western horizon, gilding heavy clouds with hues of golden splendor. Rugged hills partook of the magnificence of the sun's demise as golden rays of its passing reflected from them back into the sky. It was a scene of awesome majesty. Joseph stood there, absorbing its beauty. Heat of day soon gave way to cool breezes that stirred with coming of evening. Snapping out of his reverie, he nervously searched the areas where his brothers usually pastured the flocks. They were not there. He wondered if he had perhaps become lost. No, the familiar landmarks of Mount Gerizim and Mount Ebal stood harsh and forbidding.

While he stood, confused, an old man on a burro approached on the road from Shechem. Joseph hailed him. "Old man," he called. "I seek my brothers, the sons of Jacob. Have you heard where they pasture their flocks?"

The old man looked at him quizzically, as if admiring the brilliantly woven coat. He scratched his grizzled beard. "Your brethren pastured their flocks here, but they went to Dothan where abounded more feed for the livestock."

Joseph shook his head, watching the old man and his burro disappear down the road. How could his luck be so poor! Dothan lay another day's journey to the north. He hefted his small pack and continued wearily on his way past the fortified town of Shechem. As shadows of evening grew long, he found a spot for a camp near a small spring within sight of towering Mount Ebal. He threw down his pack and built a small fire. He made a bed in a sandy hollow where he would be protected somewhat from the wind.

By the time darkness came, a slight sprinkle fell from the heavens. Joseph sought shelter under a large sycamore tree. The sprinkle turned into a slow, steady drizzle, murmuring as it came through the leaves. Near midnight the storm broke in full force around him. Thunder rolled and rumbled like the drums of the Edomites. Great, yellow flashes of lightning made night day for long seconds. Wrapped tightly in his cloak, he huddled fearfully against the tree. Wind howled through the limbs above him, whipping against his face.

By morning, the storm disappeared, leaving only water dripping from the tree branches to remind him it had been there. The huge sycamore had protected him somewhat, but he was still soaked to the skin. Before starting out, Joseph paused for a moment in the refreshed air, bathing in the red-gold of the sky; wondering what great excitements this new day would bring.

Oh, he thought as he now sat disconsolately in the pit. If I had only known what kinds of excitements I would face on that day, I would not have started out so eagerly for Dothan.

His clothes dried quickly as he walked. By the time the hammered-gold sun stood high in the sky, Joseph climbed through the hills. He felt greatly relieved when he finally saw the broad plains of Dothan. The last time he had been here the plain resembled an undulating sea as wind passed gently through heavy heads of ripening barley. Now he shaded his eyes with his hand against the glaring sun and looked around. The valley looked flat and empty except for herds of grazing livestock. Joseph heard distant bleating of goats and barking of their guardian dogs. Nearby a solitary crow croaked its callous cry. He quickened his pace as he identified his brother's tents. Perhaps he would get there in time for supper.

From a distance he recognized his brother, Simeon. Tall and thin, Simeon walked with a limp from an injury sustained in one of his many battles. He was dark and heavily bearded, his eyes black and penetrating over dominant cheekbones and a large, hooked nose. A broad leather belt held the short bronze sword he always carried. Benjamin had once jokingly remarked that Simeon looked like a vulture ready to strike.

Reuben, Joseph's oldest brother, walked from a tent and looked towards him. Reuben was a man of medium height and powerful build. His black beard was tinged with red and gray, his eyes deep and penetrating. A leather band around his forehead held his mop of unruly hair in place. He wore a short, brown tunic with embroidered hems. A wraparound skirt, held up by a wide cloth belt, hung from his waist.

Joseph hailed them. None of his brothers returned his greeting. That surprised him. Most kept their eyes downcast, looking into the glowing embers of the fire. Even more bewildering, as Joseph arrived in their camp, Judah and Simeon grabbed him, stripped his coat from him, and against his screaming protests dragged him to the pit and lowered him into it.

Light now came into the pit from the other direction. Afternoon had come. He had been in the pit a full day. He called again. "Reuben, Judah, Levi, anyone. Please get me out of here. I promise I won't tell father." Joseph knew his brothers did not like him. What he did not know was just how much they disliked him. Before his arrival, the brothers sat cross-legged around the dying fire. Their topic of discussion, unbeknownst to them, was almost upon them.

"It was bad enough before he got that awful coat," Levi said, snapping a dry stick in his big hands. "But since then he has been impossible to live with."

Judah tore a bite from the blackened breast of the fowl roasting on a spit over the fire. Then, his mouth full, he muttered, "Even that wouldn't be so bad except he is such a bearer of tales. We can't do anything without him reporting it to Father."

Each of the brothers added comments. "He is lazy." "He walks around as if he were our leader." "Father favors him over all the rest of us." "His lofty manner shows that he thinks he is better than we are." "I don't like his insolence." The comments went on as they aired their frustrations about Joseph.

Simeon growled. "The thing that bothers me most are those silly dreams. To think he really believes that we are someday going to bow down to him like the shocks of wheat he saw in his dreams." He nodded his head. "We, who have conquered this whole land almost with our bare hands?" He laughed derisively. "I would sooner bow down to one of these cows than to that dreamer." He bowed in a mocking manner, then drank some hot broth from his bowl. "We must do something and soon," He looked meaningfully at his brothers

Judah scowled at the fire. "It cannot go on like this. Perhaps he can have an accident — one that couldn't be traced to us." Even Reuben, the oldest and quietest of the brothers, complained. "He feels superior because he is Rachel's son. He wouldn't have anything to do with us who were born of Leah or the maids." Issachar, who had been out watching the flock, came running toward them. "Brethren," he shouted. "Joseph, our brother comes. I saw his many-colored coat from afar."

His teeth bared in hatred, Simeon said, "So, the dreamer comes. What a perfect chance to kill him. We can kill him and no one will ever know. When anyone asks, we can say some wild beast must have killed him."

Heads nodded in agreement. Reuben stopped them. "No. Let us not kill him. If we did, how could we look at our father, Jacob? Rather, let's cast him into one of these empty pits where he can die and we won't have to spill his blood." Again heads nodded. It seemed a good plan. They watched as Joseph walked jauntily toward them. They could see his relief to see them after his three-day journey. "Ho, brothers," he called. "I have looked all over for you from Shechem to here. I'm surely glad I found you before another night."

Several brothers waved diffidently to him, but most averted their eyes. When he stopped, Simeon stood as if to embrace him. Instead, he grabbed him, pinning his arms to his sides. Judah pulled his legs out from under him, and then they unceremoniously dumped him onto the ground. Joseph supposed they just teased him with their play.

"Stop it," he said petulantly. Then he heard their muttered imprecations and threats. Realizing they were not playing, he twisted and turned, trying vainly to release himself from their grasp. His heart beat wildly with fear. Simeon and Judah held him securely. He tried to hold his precious coat, but to no avail. They roughly tore it from him and tied his hands behinds his back. Blows rained upon him from all directions. "There's for your dreams." "Now who is bowing down?" came shouts from his brothers as they pummeled him.

Several hands pulled him roughly to his feet where he faced the angry looks on the faces of his brothers. Now thoroughly frightened, he looked from one to another. He stood almost naked before them, with ugly welts and bruises starting to show on his face and body. Blood streamed across his chest from his nostrils, with nothing to stop the flow.

Reuben spoke. "Little brother, for the last time you have told tales about us and tried to make yourself look better than we in the eyes of our father. You deserve the punishment you are about to receive." He nodded to Simeon. "Take him away and lower him into the dry well near the hillside." He spat at the feet of his younger brother, then turned back to the fire, pretending indifference.

A cry of dread came from Joseph's throat. He kicked at those nearest him. He wriggled and squirmed, but to no avail. The brothers half-carried, half-dragged the desperately struggling and weeping Joseph to the well. Between sobs he shouted, "I swear I will not tell Father what you have done. Please let me go."

"You certainly would," Judah muttered between his teeth as he looped a rope under Joseph's arms. "That would be the first thing you would do when you got back to father's tent." He cinched the rope tightly, then, accompanied by jibes and ribald laughter from the others, lowered Joseph into the deep pit.

Chapter 2: Prisoner

Joseph shrugged in resignation. He suddenly realized how hungry he was. He fumbled at his waist-cloth and found a sticky mass of dates the ants had also found. He brushed off what he could, then ate the dates, sucking the pits until no flavor remained.

As he pulled the dates from his waistband, his fingers brushed against a smooth, round stone, the one Benjamin gave him. A wave of homesickness came over him as he thought about his brother. He wondered sadly what Benjamin was doing. The small stone represented a touch with reality. He hoarded the memories that flooded him: memories laced with food and drink, warmed by friendships, wreathed in the smells of his father's tent. With all his will, he held on to the memories. He gazed at the stone, rolled it between his palms, loved its touch. "Benjamin, will I ever see you again?" he asked aloud. He carefully replaced it in his waistband.

He felt better after eating, but thirst rasped his throat. He thought seriously about his life. *What have I done wrong? Are my brothers right to condemn me? They called me arrogant, a bearer of tales, and many other names. Father favors me, but is that terribly wrong? If I get out of this pit, what can I change to be a better son and brother?*

He remembered that when he had tended sheep with his brothers, they slipped away with some Canaanite girls. He had told his father what they had done. He nodded sadly as he thought of many such times when he had carried evil reports about his brothers to his father. *No wonder they hate me.* Then he thought of his dreams — of seeing binding sheaves in the field and how all the other sheaves had bowed down to his sheaf. He remembered how Simeon had asked scornfully, "Will you indeed reign over us?" In another dream, the sun and the moon and the eleven stars all paid homage to him. Even his father rebuked him after he told his family that dream.

As he looked back, Joseph could see that, though he had just been reporting his dreams to his family, he had shown arrogance and pride. Contritely, he knelt in dirt at the bottom of the pit, scorpions forgotten. "God of my fathers, I now see the error of my ways, and why I am being punished. If you will save me from this pit, I promise I will no longer exalt myself over my brethren but will humble myself and become their servant." He paused in his prayer as he remembered the blessing his father had given him at his bar mitzvah when he turned thirteen and attained adulthood.

Jacob presented to him the beautifully embroidered coat. "Here is a gift for you, my son," he said. "I had it made in Moriah during the feast days. The weaver had great skill."

Joseph held the coat up, turning it this way and that, very pleased with it. Then he looked at his father. "Father, how can I wear it? It is finer than any my brothers wear. They will know you gave it to me and . . ." Waving his hand impatiently, Jacob interrupted him. "I am not concerned with what Reuben and Simeon and the others think. They violated the trust I had in them. It is their fault we had to leave Shechem and move here." He gestured broadly at the narrow oasis surrounded by desert sands.

By now, Joseph had put on the coat, holding it closely to him. "It fits perfectly, father."

Jacob held him at arm's length, admiring him.

Frowning again, Joseph said, "But father, I still worry about my brothers. They hate me already. They will hate me even more when they see me wearing this coat. It will . . ."

Again Jacob interrupted. "Enough. It is yours as a symbol of your birthright. Now I desire to give you a blessing." He laid his hands on Joseph's head and blessed him: "My son, the Lord has already called you to His work. Because of your calling you have been filled with pride and have set yourself above your brothers. The Lord has great things in store for you, but he cannot bless you until you rid yourself of pride. To become a leader of men, you must first become their servant." Jacob gave him other directions for his life, then concluded: "It is a natural tendency, my son, to think of a leader as one who directs other's lives by telling them what to do, and then to accept the praise and recognition for that leadership. The Lord admonishes you that you must first think of yourself as a servant; not one who is attended to by others, but one who attends to others in such a way as to provide for their needs."

Joseph thought of the four years that had passed since that blessing. He had not obeyed his father's counsel. Pride and arrogance still represented a major part of his character. Once more tears ran down his cheeks as he considered his failure to live up to his father's blessing. *No wonder the Lord allowed me to be put in this pit!* He continued his prayer. 'God of Abraham, Isaac, and Jacob, if you will release me from this bondage, I will be humble and serve in whatever circumstance you place me." As he prayed, a feeling of peace entered his heart. It was as if a voice said to him, "Joseph, the submission of your will to God is the only uniquely personal thing you have to place on His altar. Everything else you give are things He has given you."

The brothers, not desiring to hear Joseph's screams, went off the distance of a bow shot. There, amidst the scrub oak and fig trees, they built a fire and discussed the consequences of what they had done.

Reuben would have none of the discussion. I have accomplished my purpose, he thought. At least I have gained some time and Joseph has not been killed. I will let Joseph suffer a little, then perhaps I can rescue him after dark on the morrow. Reuben thought, Perhaps this is the way to return to the good graces of Father. What if I brought Joseph safely home? Will Father forgive me for my indiscretion on account of Bilhah so many years ago? Could the curse be lifted and the blessing restored? While thinking on these things, Reuben took Dan with him and returned to the flock.

The other brothers sat eating their supper of bread and cheese. They all had different ideas about what to do with their brother.

Simeon scowled. "Let's just kill him and get it over with."

"No," Issachar pleaded. "I don't want his blood on my hands."

Zebulon, eighteen, just a year older than Joseph, also asked for leniency. "Why not just let him stay in the pit overnight, then when he is chastised enough we can take him back to our father, Jacob."

After eating, they moseyed back to their camp, still a little uneasy about what they had done; the problem of what to do with Joseph still not resolved.

Next morning the discussion continued. Some, led by Simeon, wanted to kill Joseph. Some just wanted to leave him in the pit to die of starvation and thirst. Others would pull him out of the pit and take him home. Levi listened carefully to the feelings of his brothers. He felt compassion for Joseph. He bided his time, waiting for the right moment to make his pleas. "My brothers," he began. "I can see we are not agreed as to what should be done with our arrogant little brother. I propose . . ."

He didn't get a chance to finish his proposal. An excited Napthali interrupted him. "An Ishmaelite caravan approaches."

They looked where Napthali pointed. Sure enough, a distant caravan approached on the road of Gilead. They watched silently as it drew nearer. Judah interrupted their thoughts. "My brothers," he craftily stated, "I think we have the answer to our dilemma." He looked around at his brothers. "What profit is it if we slay our brother? Instead of killing him, let's sell him to the Ishmaelites so his blood isn't on us."

Heads nodded in agreement. "Besides," Judah added. "We may make a little money in the process." Again heads nodded. Some smiled in relief that they would not have to be part of the awful task of killing their younger brother. While they waited for the distant caravan to draw nearer, they returned to their tasks of mending harness, weaving, and polishing swords and equipment.

As they sat there, seven trading men of Midian passed by on their journey eastward to Gilead. The Midianites, seeing a flock of birds circling the pit, and being very thirsty, turned towards the well, hoping to find some drinking water. Instead when they looked into the pit they saw Joseph. He looked up, and seeing the traders, knew the One God had answered his prayers.

One of the traders called. "Who are you? And how did you get into this pit?"

"I am your servant," Joseph replied. "Please pull me out and I will answer your questions."

They threw him a rope. Joseph tied it around his waist. Once again in the sunlight, he stood before them almost nude — scratched, bruised, his dusty face streaked by tears. He looked at the grim faces before him. "My brothers, angry with me, put me into the pit to punish me."

The traders looked slyly at one another. "Come, let us be on our way," said one who seemed to be the leader. They loaded the unprotesting Joseph onto a pack camel and were ready to resume their journey when Joseph's brothers caught up with them.

Judah shouted. "Why do you steal our servant? We placed this youth in the pit because he rebelled against us. Now you bring him up and lead him away. Give us back our servant."

The Midianite, a large man with flowing black beard, replied curtly. "Your story makes no sense. Perhaps you are servants to this youth and attempted to do away with him." He noticed the covert glances between several of the brothers and knew he had hit upon a grain of truth. "He is more comely and well-favored than any of you. Why do you speak falsely to us?" The other traders nodded in agreement. "Besides, we found him in the pit. He is now our property. We will take him and do with him what we want." He pulled the camel around and started to turn back to the trail.

Simeon grabbed the rope, pulling the camel up short. He demanded hotly, "Return our servant or die by the sword."

The Midianites drew their swords. Joseph, confused and frightened, looked from the traders to his brothers, wondering what he should do. Simeon dropped the camels rope. He stepped back, bronze sword held high. He shouted. "I am Simeon, son of Jacob, the Hebrew." He pointed to Levi. "My brother and I destroyed the city of Shechem and the cities of the Amorites. Give us back the youth you have taken, or I will give your flesh to the birds and beasts."

Cowed, the Midianite returned his sword to his belt. "You said the young man is a rebellious servant. Why not sell him to us?"

Simeon looked at Judah who nodded his head almost imperceptibly. Turning back to the traders, Simeon said, "Twenty pieces of silver and he's yours."

"Khikkh," the Midianite commanded. The camel knelt. The Midianite reached into his pouch, bringing out a handful of silver. On a small balance scale he carefully weighed out twenty shekels.

Joseph sat on the pack camel, tongue-tied and wide-eyed. Were his brothers really selling him? He started to protest, then bowed his head, remembering the promise he had made to the Lord "... a servant in all circumstances." He held his tongue.

Payment made, the Midianite remounted and turned east with his fellow traders. Joseph looked back. His brothers stood shoulder to shoulder, watching him go. The Midianites traveled only a short distance when one asked, "Do you think we did right?"

"What do you mean?"

"Perhaps this youth is stolen from the land of the Hebrews. If so, and they find him in our hands, they will kill us."

Another nodded. "They who sold him were hardy and powerful. If they stole him from this land and sold him for such a paltry sum, surely someone will come looking for the lad."

As they discussed what to do, the Ishmaelite caravan approached. "Let's sell him to the Ishmaelites," one said. "Then we will be free of any evil he may bring."

The Ishmaelite caravan stopped for the night. Camel drivers unloaded boxes of gum, fragrant balm, and rare spices from the East. They set boxes of Syrian wares carefully on the ground. The Midianites threaded through the large caravan, finally locating the caravan master. When they approached him with an offer to buy the handsome Joseph, he accepted gladly. The lad would bring a good price in the Egyptian slave market. He paid the Midianites their twenty shekels of silver.

Darkness blanketed the two silent figures. Reuben leaned over the dark pit, calling softly, "Joseph. Joseph." No response. Fearful that Joseph had died of fright or that some serpent had bitten him, Reuben tied a rope around Dan and lowered him into the pit.

"There is no one here!" Dan called. "The pit is empty. Joseph has vanished." Reuben pulled Dan to the surface, then symbolically, tore the hem of his robe. They made their way back to camp, where the brothers sat gloomily around the fire.

"Dan and I went to see Joseph," Reuben announced. "He is gone. I don't know how he got out of the well, but he has disappeared." He looked around at his brothers. "What will we tell father? As the oldest he will turn to me and ask what happened to his son."

The brothers refused to look at him but continued to stare into the fire. Judah leaned on his staff nearest Reuben. All looked guilty. Reuben looked around at them, then grabbed Judah by his robe with both hands. He pulled him until they stood face to face. "What have you done to Joseph?" he shouted.

Simeon jumped up and separated his brothers. "Let me tell you," he said. He recounted all that had happened, then added lamely, "We are sorry for what we did."

"Sorry!" Reuben shouted. "Being sorry won't help now. What you have done is to send our father to his grave."

"No!" Judah cried, springing to his feet. "No one must tell him what happened. We must all swear not to tell."

Levi interposed. "Let us take an oath. If any man tells what happened we will slay him."

For some time it was quiet at the campfire. Judah looked around the circle of faces illuminated by the flickering fire. "We must tell father something. How can we explain Joseph's disappearance?" Issachar said, "Let's take Joseph's coat, tear it, and kill a goat and dip the coat in its blood. Then we can send it to father who will think a wild beast devoured him."

Heads nodded. A murmur of acceptance of Issachar's proposal passed through the group. Dan left to kill a kid. When he returned they tore Joseph's beautiful coat, dipped it into the goat's blood and tramped it into the dust.

The brothers selected Napthali, smoothest talker in the family, to take Joseph's coat to Jacob. Judah coached him. "Tell Father we had gathered in the cattle and started home when we found this coat upon the road to Shechem. It looked like Joseph's, so I brought it home to you."

Napthali nodded, and carrying the bloody coat, loped off toward Mamre.

Chapter 3: Journey to Egypt

About the time the brothers started south with their herds of kine and goats, the Ishmaelite caravan resumed its long journey toward Egypt. Joseph, son of Jacob, clothed in a rough goats-hair coat, rode a pack camel. As the ponderous caravan slowly got under way, Joseph looked at his people's land of promise and wondered if this would be the last time he would see it. Sighing deeply, he resigned himself to whatever fate the One God had in store for him.

The caravan followed the same trail Joseph had traveled from Hebron to Dothan. By afternoon, the long, winding procession reached Shechem. Joseph again looked at the two mountains which overlooked the valley: Mount Gerizim with its green, tree-covered slopes, and nearby Mount Ebal, always bleak and desolate. He compared the two mountains to his life. Just a few days before he had been like Mount Gerizim — full of life and promise. Now Mount Ebal seemed more to symbolize his life — desolate of spirit, despairing, with little hope for the future. He shook his shoulders violently. *No, he said to himself. I cannot let self pity control my thoughts. The Lord controls what happens. It is in His hands. I must remove all doubt and discouragement from my mind I will let go of the past and let God control my life.*

The caravan snaked its way past Shechem along the mountainous trail. Joseph gazed longingly at this land of his youth. It was October — the time of nature's rebirth. The first rain — the one his people called the yoreh — had come to Canaan, signaling that wild fruits and berries would now be ripe. He thought of the many times he had wandered the hills picking the pears, hawthorn, and arbutus. Soon the crocus would poke its green spears through the ground. Wild grasses would come forth in the bottoms and the prairies. Cylamen and narcissus would cover the hillsides. This was his father's and grandfather's land of promise.

For Joseph, it no longer represented a land of promise. No more would he be free to roam the hills at his leisure. No more would he lie on his back in the shade of a fig tree watching the procession of clouds marching valiantly across his sky. *I am a slave!* The word stuck in his throat. He had watched gangs of slaves herded down the dusty road to Egypt. Now he was one of them — a nameless one. Oh, how he already missed his freedom. He murmured to himself: *I did not value my freedom until it was taken from me.*

The caravan camped the first night at Lebonah, about midway between Shechem and Bethel. The Ishmaelite guard gave Joseph a few dates for his supper, then trussed him again, binding his arms together at the elbows. The rope cut cruelly across his back. Being tied up made him feel lower than the goats kept tied behind his father's tent. He let his emotions go. Tears rolled down his cheeks in the dark. Self-pity again engulfed him. He felt so empty and alone. Shifting his position, he looked up into the heavens. *Why? Why? Lord, are you continuing to punish me for my past mistakes?*

As soon as the camp was quiet, Joseph leaned his back against a rock and sawed back and forth, hoping to wear through the thick cord. After an hour all he had succeeded in doing was scraping the sores on his arms, causing them to bleed. But the rope held. As the half moon set in the west, he fell into a fitful sleep, his dreams unclear and jumbled. First he saw his brothers, their faces grotesque as they mocked him. His dreams shifted to his father. He saw him, an embroidered coat in his hands, weeping over the loss of his favorite son.

Joseph cried out in his sleep. The guard at the fire walked over, looked down upon the sleeping youth and whacked him across the back with his staff. Joseph cried out in pain and looked up fearfully. The guard, outlined against the flickering fire, stood there black and silent. Joseph trembled from fright and cold, curling his knees up as high as he could against his chest. Without speaking, the guard walked back to the fire. Joseph lay awake, praying silently to the One God.

At dawn, his muscles refused to respond. The tight bonds had cut off his circulation. He had a difficult time standing, but under the prod of the guard stumbled over to help load the camels. As he worked, thoughts of his father filled his mind. The caravan would soon be passing Hebron and the oasis of Mamre where his father dwelt. Tears flowed again.

The driver, seeing the tears, cursed him, then beat Joseph across the back with his prod. "Ho, weak Hebrew. What are these? Tears of shame for being such a weakling?" He struck him again. "I'll teach you to weep." He grabbed Joseph, and with a stout cord, roughly tied his hands together in front. The other end of the cord he tied to the camel's harness. Other drivers gathered around, taunting Joseph. "We will see how well he walks," the driver shouted. Others laughed.

As the camel started forward, Joseph stumbled along the rocky trail. He tried to keep his balance, dodging the larger stones. Then he tripped and fell headlong, pulled along behind the camel until he regained his footing. Fall and get up. Fall and get up. Within an hour he was totally fatigued, bruised and bloody, his clothes reduced to rags. He fell again.

Almost unconscious, he let the camel drag him along the beaten trail. The camel driver stopped the camel and stalked back with his prod. He struck Joseph repeatedly across the shoulders and back.

The caravan master, coming upon the scene, wrenched the prod from the driver. "Would you decrease the value of this slave by ruining his beauty?" Lifting the limp and barely conscious Joseph, they put him on the camel. He lurched from side to side with the animal's sway. As the sun dipped below the western hills, the caravan reached a lovely hillside oasis. Joseph, conscious again, looked around. Ephrath. The place where his mother lay buried. He bowed his head and fought back his tears.

A voice came into his mind, almost as if his mother spoke to him. "Go willingly down to Egypt with your masters. Do not fear. I, the Lord, am with you."

* * *

Napthali, quick of foot, far outdistanced both the caravan and his brothers with their livestock. Panting and exhausted, he arrived at his father's tent. Without taking time to rest, he entered the patriarchal tent and prostrated himself before Jacob. "My father," he gasped. "While traveling through the valley of Shechem, we found this coat. I brought it to you because we did not know if it belonged to your son, Joseph."

At sight of the blood-stiffened rags which had once been a coat, Jacob fell to his knees. He took the rag in his hands. Head bowed to the earth, he moaned. "It is Joseph's coat. Wild beasts must have devoured him. Oh, my Joseph!" Beating his head on the hard earth, he moaned aloud. With both hands he reached down to the hem of his garment and tore it.

Napthali felt helpless as he watched his father's grief. Pains of guilt churned inside him.

Eliazar, Jacob's personal servant, motioned. He and Napthali picked up Jacob and carried him to his bed. Jacob's eyes remained closed, his breathing shallow and quick. Except for the moans and prayers coming from his lips, he appeared as if in a coma. Napthali sensed his father's abject suffering. Jacob had lost his favorite wife. Now he had lost the son who reminded him so much of that wife.

"He is dead! He is dead!" Jacob moaned. Glassy-eyed and sightless, he lay on his pallet. Jacob did not eat for three days, refusing even the broth Bilhah offered. On the fourth day he arose, shuffled to the dead firepit before the tent, sat down, and symbolically poured ashes over his uncovered head. His grief expurgated, he allowed himself to be led into his tent where Eliazar cleaned him up. Jacob prayed, "Oh, God, though You have snatched my son from me, Your will be done. But please, God," he prayed, "let me see my son again someday."

* * *

Camels watered, the caravan's snail-like journey continued. Joseph, still not sure of the One God's plans for him, made one more attempt to free himself from his masters. As they rode past Hebron and the oasis at Mamre, he pleaded with the caravan master. "Oh sir, if you will but take me to my father's tent, he will reward you with riches."

The master looked sardonically at the youth. "You are but a slave. Slaves do not have fathers or mothers. If you had a father you would not already have been sold twice as a slave for so little value!" He laughed at his own cleverness, slashing Joseph across the cheek with his whip.

Tearfully, Joseph looked over his shoulder until the oasis faded from sight. He thought again of what the voice had said. "Go willingly down to Egypt with your masters. Do not fear. I, the Lord, am with you." Finally understanding that the Lord, for some reason, wanted him in Egypt, Joseph straightened his shoulders and clamped his teeth tightly together. He said determinedly to himself, *I will weep no more. From this time forward I will trust in the Lord and obey his every command. I will let Him direct me wherever He wants me to go.* His fingers strayed to his waistband. He fondled the small stone — his only possession — a reminder of family and home.

By the time they reached Beersheba, darkness had fallen. The land through which they traveled had grown perceptibly less green since leaving Hebron. Palm trees were a welcome sight against the night sky. The caravan camped around a beautiful spring fringed with spreading acacias and date palms. The driver untied Joseph to let him eat a meager supper, then re-tied him. Joseph , instead of lying there feeling sorry for himself, looked around. He realized that from the moment his brothers put him into the pit, his thoughts had been on himself and his terrible plight. Now, he became aware of others. *The best way I can serve the One God,* he thought, *is to take my eyes off myself and put them on others.* He took note of his surroundings. The size of the caravan amazed him. From where he lay he could see the glare and rising smoke from scores of small fires. Few tents had been put up, but slaves had erected a goats-hair tent for the caravan overseer.

Somewhat timidly, he called, "Ho, guard."

The camel driver looked up, his eyes unused to the dark beyond the fire. He turned his head, then settled back into his slumped position. Again Joseph called, this time more boldly. "Ho, guard, I desire to talk with you."

The guard stood and stretched. He stopped about ten feet short of Joseph, leaning on his almond staff. "What do you want, slave?"

Speaking slowly, Joseph replied. "I wish to covenant with you. If you remove these cords which bind me, I promise I will not attempt to escape, but will go willingly with you to Egypt."

Grunting, the guard spat upon the ground, turned, and walked to the tent of the overseer. A blazing torch signaled his return.

"What is this you ask?" The overseer's tone was suspicious.

"I have made my peace with my God," Joseph looked up from where he lay. "I pledge to you not to attempt to escape if you will remove these bonds. Then I will be better able to serve you."

The overseer looked at him, then nodded at the driver. Sneering at the youth on the ground, the guard loosed the cords. They dropped to the sand as Joseph massaged his sore elbows. The overseer returned to his tent.

Joseph looked at the man who had been guarding him. Swallowing hard, he knelt in the sand before him. "Sir, I am your servant. What will you have me do?"

The guard looked amazed. Was this self-assured young man the same one that had sniveled and whined for the past three days? He shrugged and strode back to the fire. Joseph followed at a respectful distance. "Sir," he repeated. "How may I serve you?"

"We need fuel for the fire," the guard responded gruffly.

Joseph slipped away. Within minutes he returned with an armful of dried camel droppings. Depositing them by the fire, he again left. This time he returned with sticks that could be used as kindling for the morning fire. The guard watched him suspiciously as he came and went. When Joseph had a good supply of chips and wood by the fire, the guard motioned with his hand, "Sit here."

Joseph obediently sat. The guard stirred the fire with his stick, sending a shower of sparks upward into the night sky. The two silently looked at the fire. Without looking at Joseph, the guard said, "I am Akdar."

"And I am called Joseph."

The fire burned to red coals winking on and off in the pit. Joseph lay down in the sand a short distance away and, exhausted, soon slept. Akdar yawned, stood, and went to his pallet. In a few minutes he returned with his pack. He pulled out a blanket and covered the young slave.

Chapter 4: Across the Desert

The caravan remained in Beersheba for several days. The caravan master seemed in no hurry to leave Beersheba — the last halting place before the desert. Joseph kept busy filling water jugs. Camels and drivers rested in preparation for the inhospitable desert which lay before them.

As they sat around the fire in the evenings, Akdar told Joseph of the desert, of its miles of dry and dusty sand in which nothing lived save a few sparse patches of wretched scrub. He hold him of sand so hot it burned right through the leather soles of their sandals. He told of times when people just gave up in the desert, lay down in the sand, and let its burning end their lives — their parched lips and dried out skins becoming one with their bleached bones.

Joseph roamed throughout the huge encampment, noting the camels with their gaily-decorated headstalls and harness. For the first time he saw the diverse colors and races of the people. The Ishmaelites, large, black-bearded men, burned dark by the ever-glaring sun, wore ankle-length striped burnoose which reached to the ankles. White linen head-bands, held in place with black felt circlets, protected heads and faces from the sun. The camel drivers, including Akdar, were a breed unto themselves: small, wiry, brown men, scantily clothed in loincloths, high-piled turbans, and goat-leather sandals. They seemed almost immune to the burning desert sun. Faces were hairless and wrinkled. Deep-set black eyes constantly squinted.

Joseph noticed other slaves in the caravan. Most had no sandals. Joseph marveled at how tough their feet must be to walk across the burning sand. The female slaves seemed well-muscled and sturdy. They kept to themselves, eyes downcast, seeming to accept their miserable lot. While at the spring he met a merchant traveling north. Taking a scrap of scroll he found and a piece of charcoal from the firepit, Joseph wrote his father, telling him all that had happened to him — his trip to Dothan, the pit, and the caravan. He gave the scroll to the merchant. "Please take this to my father, Jacob, at Mamre."

The third day they broke camp. Slaves struck the few tents, drivers loaded recalcitrant camels and donkeys, and everyone filled water jugs for the last time. Two of the wetly shining goatskins hung from the camel on which Joseph rode. Their bloated, black, slippery sides felt cool to the touch.

As the caravan moved across the unfamiliar desert terrain south of Beersheba, Joseph looked back for the last time at the land of his inheritance. His thoughts dwelt on his father — with hope he had received his message.

Days blurred in Joseph's mind. Few wells existed in the great expanse of sand and rock, and even in October the sun beat mercilessly down upon the earth. Akdar told Joseph the trail they followed was called the Way to Shur. A day's journey beyond Beersheba the trail forked. The left trail led straight across the desert, but the caravan master turned to the trail on the right, called The Way of the Land of the Philistines. Joseph could not see that it made any difference. The barren, sandy plain and rock-covered hills stretched as far as he could see in any direction. Sometimes they camped at springs, but most camps had no water, sheltered only by dunes of blowsand.

The desert through which they passed remained monotonous: sand dunes, rocks, low-rolling hills, and more sand dunes. Red cliffs glittered on the horizon to the south, fading into distant ghostly purple peaks,. Sandstone rocks took grotesque shapes from the constant eroding wind. Heat shimmered above the sand, giving impression of distant lakes. Sand penetrated nose, ears, mouth, eyes.

Each night by the fire, Akdar told Joseph of other journeys across this desert, of sandstorms, and of raids by nomads he called "desert sand rabbits." These nomads swept down upon caravans from the shelter of dunes to pillage and steal. But on this journey, nothing oppressed them but sand and sun and wind and heat. The slow swaying rhythm of the camel and the constant heat often lulled Joseph to sleep. He dozed and dreamed of the past. His mind went back ten years to that other great caravan of which he had been a part.

* * *

His father, Jacob, left Haran and journeyed to the promised land. Joseph, just seven, felt the excitement of the journey: wagons filled with women and little children, pack burros, great flocks and herds following closely behind the wagons. Freight wagons followed the flocks. He recalled how his grandfather, Laban, caught up with them and searched through everything, looking for his idols. He had been angry.

The most exciting part of the journey had been the meeting of his father and his Uncle Esau. Joseph rode in the wagon with his mother while the older brothers rode horses, driving the herds and flocks. They bumped along in the slow-moving cart with his Aunt Leah driving the team of oxen. He sat in the rear, behind the rolled-up tent, his legs dangling over the back. Occasionally, when no one was looking, he jumped off the wagon, picked up some small stones, then jumped back on. He threw the stones at rocks and clumps of brush to pass the time.

Fast hoof beats diverted him from his boredom. He turned to see his father, Jacob, riding up. Jacob leaned over and gave Rachel a resounding kiss, causing her to blush. Joseph stood up in the rocking wagon, stepping forward to his father. Jacob reached down, circled Joseph's waist with his large arm, and adroitly lifted him out of the wagon and set him in front of him on the horse.

His mother looked at Jacob, a question in her eyes. "Where . . ."

Jacob cut her off. "Don't worry. I will just take him for a short ride."

"But what of Esau? I thought . . ."

"Simeon sent back word that Esau will meet us this afternoon." Joseph, astride the horse, looked up at his father. A look of worry crossed Jacob's ruggedly handsome but wrinkled face.

Rachel, too, noticed the frown. "What is it, my dear?"

"I cannot understand why Esau has so many men with him. Issachar scouted them and says there are over four hundred!" He paused in thought, then continued. "Unless he intends to do battle."

A shocked gasp came from Rachel. "What will you do?"

Jacob smiled. "I have taken care of it," he said. "Reuben and Levi have cut out almost half of our herd and are taking them forward as a gift for my brother." He mused, almost to himself. "He always liked to take the easy way out. I do not think he will want to battle us."

Joseph continued looking up at his father. Jacob glanced down at his seven-year-old. With his free hand he tousled Joseph's hair and waved at Rachel. Joseph was excited. His father was taking him to meet Esau, the wild and hairy uncle he had been told so much about. He could feel the nervousness of his father — or was it just excitement like his own?

Neither Jacob nor Joseph spoke as they rode. Joseph felt content just to feel the warmth and love of his father near him. At last they caught up with the other brothers and the large flock of goats and herds of kine. Dust filled the air. Joseph's bottom smarted from the horse's sharp backbone, but he didn't complain. He rode contentedly until his father said, "Look!"

He peered around the neck and head of the horse. Desert Bedouins rode toward them, led by a large, red-haired man on a beautiful white horse. It must be his Uncle Esau. Joseph's father signaled the other sons to stay with the herd, then rode forward alone, except for seven-year-old

Joseph on the saddle with him.

Esau, a big man whose mane of red hair showed a weaving of gray, sat on his horse as if he were a part of it. Joseph had never seen such a horse: soft white in color, its eyes and the insides of its ears were pink! He stared at the horse, memorizing every detail — each rippling muscle and sleek line. As he looked at the beautiful and sensitive animal, he made a childish resolve that someday he would have a horse just like that — a white one with pink eyes and ears. He became aware of his father's voice.

"Thank you, my brother. It has been many years. We will cross the Jordan and settle there with your blessings. And father . . .?"

"He lives," the red-haired uncle replied. "But he is too weak to travel. He awaits you at the oasis of Mamre." He paused, apparently noticing Joseph for the first time. "And who is this?"

Joseph felt himself being picked up off the saddle. With a quick shove, his father catapulted him into the air, and before he could gasp or yell, he found himself caught by those large red-hairy arms. His Uncle Esau held him up and looked him in the eyes. Then he turned to Jacob. "A comely lad. Your youngest?"

Smiling, Jacob nodded. "Yes, son of my favored wife, Rachel, whom I will have you meet."

Effortlessly, Esau tossed Joseph back to his father, who promptly placed him again on the saddle before him. Engrossed in the beautiful horse before him, Joseph heard little of the conversation. Snatches penetrated his consciousness: "settle down;" "Canaan;" "king;" "army." He could feel his father's happiness over this reunion with a long-separated brother, but the rest of the conversation eluded him. He loved his father dearly and enjoyed sitting on the saddle with him.

* * *

The camel stopped its swaying walk, bringing Joseph back to the present. Blinking several times to get used to the burning glare, he squinted his eyes. The caravan had ground to a halt. Camels placidly chewed their cuds, heads held high. At the front of the caravan Joseph made out the green of palm trees outlined against drabness of sand dunes. An oasis! South of the oasis, dunes rose sharply to the sky. Joseph could see walls of dry, brown mountains. He called to Akdar,

"What is it? Where are we?"

Akbar didn't even look at him. "We are at the Place of the Small Spring." He gestured towards the hills. "These hills are called Jebel

Helal and Jebel Yeleq. Travelers call them the watchmen of the desert."

Joseph helped unload and bed down the camels. By the time slaves and drivers finished their tasks, supper fires threw sparks to the sky and dusk settled on the camp. A rising wind, blowing down the canyon from the hills, whipped at Joseph's face. He ducked his head to avoid sharp sand particles. Akdar, his face masked by the cowl of his hood, smiled. "You are not used to the desert."

It was not a question, but a statement of fact. Joseph turned, his head still lowered. "Can anyone get used to such a place?" He thought of the greenery of the land he had left. "How can anyone live here?" He motioned to the Bedouin tents surrounding the water holes.

Akdar said, "Every man must have his homeland."

Sadness filled Joseph's mind as he realized he no longer did. Kitterah, son of the caravan master, hurried towards them, interrupting his thoughts.

"My father would see you in his tent."

Joseph bowed. "His wish is my command." He would have liked to take time to wash in one of the cool-looking water holes, but he followed Kitterah to his tent.

The master, Balshazar, sat on his mat in the low entrance of his traveling tent. He held a piece of papyrus. Joseph's heart sank — the letter he had written to his father. He approached the master and bowed low, eyes downcast. "You summoned me, master?"

With a wave of the scroll, Balshazar motioned Joseph to sit. Joseph hastened to obey, his heart beating rapidly. The master looked steadily at Joseph. "You can read and write?" Joseph nodded.

Balshazar stroked his beard, his black eyes boring into the tall, slender youth. "In my country, only scribes know how to read and write. Do you possess these skills? Were you trained as a scribe?"

"No, the scribe of my father taught me."

Remembering Joseph's earlier request to be turned over to his father, the master asked, "And who is your father?"

Joseph squared his shoulders and looked Balshazar in the eye. "My father is Jacob, the Hebrew Patriarch. He dwells in the oasis at Mamre near Hebron." His voice rang with quiet assurance.

Balshazar shook his head. "I know not of your father." He paused, then asked. "But if your father is a man of wealth and power, as you say, why is it that you were sold as a slave?"

Feeling tears, Joseph swallowed and looked down. He started to say,

"My brothers, resentful that I held the birthright, sold me to the Midianite traders." Instead, he looked into Balshazar's eyes and said, "I was arrogant. My brothers hated me. Now I am here in your service."

Balshazar nodded knowingly. Selling one's relatives into slavery was not a rarity in his land. "Do you also cipher and keep books?"

"I kept the records of my father."

"Good." Balshazar rubbed his hands together gleefully. "You will bring a high price in the slave market." Then another thought struck him. "You will help me with the caravan records."

"As you desire, master."

Balshazar clapped his hands. An attractive young slave appeared from within the tent. Joseph glanced up at her. He had never been around many girls. His sister, Dinah, was much older than he and there were few girls at Mamre. This girl, probably fourteen or fifteen, barefoot, wore only a loin skirt around her waist. She stopped before Balshazar, her chin almost resting on her chest. Light from the lamp in the tent danced over her features, illuminating the lovely olive sheen of her skin. When she looked up, dark almond-shaped eyes picked up the flickering of the flames.

"Bring supper," Balshazar curtly ordered.

The slave girl bowed and returned to the cool darkness of the tent. Joseph, curious now, watched her. From a goatskin bag hanging in a corner, she took rich cheese curd. She slopped these onto clay platters, then placed several small loaves of bread on each platter. Joseph became aware of Balshazar talking.

". . . Because you help me with my records, you will live in my tent for the rest of the journey to Egypt. Other slaves can help Akdar with the camels." He stopped talking and licked his lips as the girl set a platter on the mat before them.

Joseph mimicked his host, dipping bread in the cheese curd. The slave girl brought a partially- filled goatskin of water and hung it on the door post. His mouth full of bread and cheese, Balshazar talked on. Joseph listened politely. He had been unaware of her approach, but the slave girl stood beside him with a tray of dried raisins, dates, and figs. He took a handful of raisins from the tray, looked up and smiled at the girl, and continued listening.

After they had eaten, Balshazar curtly dismissed him with instructions to bring his belongings to the tent. Joseph returned to where Akdar sat by his fire. Joseph hated to leave this man who had once been cruel to him, but was now his friend. He told Akdar what had happened at the tent of the master, then picked up the few clothes which had been given him since his purchase and returned to the master's tent.

Balshazar was gone. Joseph unrolled his pallet in the corner of the tent where Balshazar had indicated he would sleep. He noticed the slave girl, retired now to the women's quarters behind the tent partition. She watched him. He sat down on the pallet. "What is your name?" he asked. The curtain abruptly closed, but in a moment it cracked open again. A shy voice responded, "I am called Desir."

"Day-Seer. That is a pretty name. Why are you here as a slave?"

"Bedouins stole me from the house of my father in Beth-Arbel. Balshazar bought me from those who stole me." Tears glistened in her dark eyes. Joseph, seeing her thus silently weeping, stood to console her. She drew back, closing the curtain.

"Are you afraid of me?" he called through the curtain.

A sob shook her voice. "I fear all men."

"I would not harm you. I am a slave like you."

Balshazar's portly figure filled the entrance, ending their conversation. Joseph determined to get better acquainted with the girl. He had never seen anyone so lovely.

The next few days Joseph rode close to the front of the caravan. Now that he managed Balshazar's affairs, people treated him differently. He took responsibility not only for the records, but also for his master's tent. He gained Desir's confidence. Sadly, she recounted the tale of her capture. With downcast eyes she told him of losing not only her freedom, but also her virtue to the slave traders. Joseph did not know what to say. He turned away and prayed silently, *Father, please help me help Desir.*

In the relative coolness of evening, they walked through the camp. He turned to her. "What you tell saddens me. It is difficult for me to understand how men can be so cruel."

Fists clenched, she cried out. "Men are without compassion."

Joseph took her hand. "Not all men. My father taught me that we are the children of God. Because some men have departed from His teachings they have become cruel and unfeeling."

"Children of God?" She rolled the question on her tongue.

"Yes. My father taught me that each of us is a child of God. God is our Father."

Desir laughed derisively. "My people's god is a bull. I do not want to be a child of that god."

"The One God," Joseph tried to explain, "is a loving father. He has compassion for those who sorrow." He could see it was a new concept for Desir and that she had difficulty understanding it.

"Why would such a God allow us to be torn from our homes and sold into slavery? Why would he allow men to . . .?"

"I don't know why. But I believe He has a purpose for us. If we bear up under afflictions He will use us to fulfill His purposes."

She looked at him in puzzlement. "I must lose my freedom to fulfill the purposes of your God?"

Struggling for words to express himself, Joseph responded helplessly. "I am not sure why some things happen." A new thought hit him. "Everyone has problems or troubles of some kind. It is how we handle those problems that counts. You and I have lost our physical freedom. Just like you, my freedom was precious to me. I have determined if a person has his freedom he should not complain about anything." He paused to collect his thoughts. "No matter what happens to our physical freedom, a person always has the freedom of his own mind — to dream, to plan, to think his own thoughts. No slave master can take that away from you."

They walked silently through the camp. Desir shyly took his hand. "I do not understand all you say, but now I feel a measure of peace I have not felt since my capture."

That night as Joseph knelt in prayer, he asked: "Why? Why are people so cruel to each other? My father taught me that we are Your children. Why should Your children do such things?"

He lay awake, eyes open and staring. The only relief of the tent's blackness was the hint of starlight outlining the open door. Restless, his mind still troubled, he rolled from one side to the other. Again, he felt the stillness which seemed to precede answers to prayer. It was a feeling of calmness — of peace. Again he heard the still, small voice. "If you are faithful, through you I will once again establish a mighty people. You will be instrumental in helping me fulfill the blessing I gave your great-grandfather, Abraham. Through you his seed will be blessed."

Joseph did not know what to think. *Here I am, but a seventeen-year-old youth, and the Lord is telling me I will be a leader of His people.* He shook his head in wonderment. "Father, I promise You I will be faithful." He thought of Desir's forced loss of virtue. "I will be chaste before You. I promise You, Father, that my mind and heart will remain pure."

Again a warmth — a feeling of vibrating silence permeated his being. It was as if the Lord responded: "That is well, my son."

The caravan entered a part of the desert where flat-topped hills, jutting spikes, and towering pillar rocks resembled the floor of a dried out ocean. Grotesque gardens of white chalk, wind-carved statues, gleaming in fields of gray dust, dotted the barren landscape. Mountains of sand seemed to be slowly swallowing whole buttes and mesas as endless dunes undulated like frozen gold waves into the cloudless blue horizon. The desert, harsh and forbidding, still had an eerie beauty. Small clumps of grass and occasional flowers struggled for life. Spiders and lizards burrowed into the sand to escape the heat. The marked contrast of day's heat and night's cold surprised Joseph. One day, in the distance, Joseph saw a dust storm. In one moment it obliterated the sky — huge boiling brown clouds rising from the earth in ever-mushrooming crescendos until brown of dust met white of clouds high in the heavens. Joseph could not find words to describe the sight. It was as if the very bowels of the earth exploded into the sky. Overhead the sun moved dimly through the pale yellow haze. On the thirteenth day after leaving Beersheba, breastworks of large stone buildings rose in the distance. Joseph looked at Balshazar, a question in his expression.

"Ah, the Egyptian border station of Khetem," Balshazar said. "We must pass through the Egyptian guards here. It is the place of the bitter lakes. From here it is only four days to Memphis."

As they approached the border station, Joseph gazed in awe at the huge buildings. His life had been lived in a world of tents. Even small villages had few buildings and those were tiny and made of mud and stone. Here Joseph saw bastions, breastworks and watchtowers extending far into the desert. Companies of soldiers manned the walls: Nubian bowmen with ostrich feathers in their hair; Libyan ax-bearers, and Egyptian soldiers with armor and metal helmets. To Joseph, it was an awesome sight. More than the sight of it, however, was the thought that from here he would be in the land of the underworld — the land of the dead about which his father had spoken in hushed tones. From here on there was no turning back.

Desir, seeming to read his thoughts, looked up. She asked softly, "Joseph, Balshazar has given you much freedom. Why have you not tried to escape?" Joseph looked down with compassion at the slight girl standing in the hot sand. "I cannot escape. I gave my word."

He thought of how Jacob had taught him that a man's word was his bond, that he would rather lose his freedom than his integrity. Thinking of his father again brought painful memories. He wondered what his father was doing. And Benjamin? Tears burned his eyes as he thought of his younger brother whom he had sworn to protect. As he looked up at the huge stone walls with the soldiers on top, he wondered if he would ever see his family again. He reached into his waist band and rolled the small stone around in his fingers.

Border guards bought Balshazar's trade goods and Joseph sat nearby keeping track of all the petty transactions. His work pleased Balshazar. That night in the tent he looked at the journal entries Joseph had made. "No blots," he exclaimed. "My records have never looked so good. And I have never received such good prices for my goods! he continued. "You have certainly brought good luck to me and the caravan." He paused in thought, pursing his lips and unconsciously sucking on his whiskers. As Joseph watched, he seemed to come to a decision. Joseph waited patiently. "Joseph," Balshazar began, "you are too valuable to be put on the auction block where just anyone can buy you." He lapsed into silence. "I know someone who can use your talents. He is a distant cousin of mine." Joseph looked up, a question in his eyes.

Balshazar smiled and continued. "Warrior Semite tribes of Arabia swept from the north fifty years ago. They conquered not only your land but the land of Egypt as well. Egyptians called them the 'shepherd king', the 'Hyksos'. Though they adopted Egyptian gods and customs, they are still our relatives and friendly to our people." he mused. "My cousin is Potiphar, the captain of Pharoah's guard." He smiled again. "He could use a servant like you."

Chapter 5: In Egypt

"That one over there." The overseer pointed with the butt of his whip. "The one with the reddish blonde hair — the young one. Where is he from?"

"Oh," Balshazar said. "That's Joseph. We call him the dreamer. He's from up north in Canaan. Claims to be the son of a rich desert sheik."

Amunkhum, the overseer of the slave auction, guffawed. "They all make claims. We have a proverb here. Every slave in the world is of royal blood." He looked admiringly at the comely, blue-eyed youth. "I can get a good price for him." He nudged the fat caravan master in the ribs. "Many men like to buy handsome boys."

Balshazar didn't look at him. "Joseph's not for sale on your auction block. I will take personal care of his sale."

While this conversation went on, the object of their discussion stood distraught at the side of the square. That human beings could be sold like so many cattle or sheep still stretched Joseph's comprehension. A small platform stood in the center of the square before him, raised above the crowd of buyers and onlookers. On the platform a dark Egyptian, dressed in white linen, auctioned off a black Nubian. Joseph watched sadly as the Egyptian paraded one slave after another across the auction block. As they stepped onto the block, the auctioneer cruelly stripped off their clothes, forcing them to stand nude before the crowd. When they dragged Desir to the platform, Joseph turned away. He could not bear to watch the humiliation of the girl who had become his friend.

He heard the auctioneer's singsong voice as he echoed the bids. Not far from Joseph, an Egyptian, muscular and bare-chested, wearing a short skirt of embroidered linen, raised his hand languidly to signal his bid. Joseph walked further away, but not far enough to avoid hearing the cry of "sold." He turned and watched dejectedly as a bald, pudgy, and very florid-faced man pulled the naked Desir from the stand. The man wore a leather apron over his large paunch and looked like a tavern owner. What a miserable fate for such a lovely girl, Joseph thought sadly. He could hardly see his ledger through teary eyes, but he made one last entry: "Desir . . . 60 pieces of copper."

The auction continued, but Balshazar's slaves, except for himself, had all been sold. He rolled up the ledger, stuck it under his arm, and sat on a step waiting for his master. He watched the newly purchased slaves led away by their owners, many tied or in chains. Thanks be to the One

God at least I don't have to be bound, he thought. He shook his head as another thought hit him. Many people are bound by their own negative thoughts — and those thoughts can be more binding then metal chains. Joseph closed his eyes and resolved once again to approach his future with faith — faith in the One God, and faith in himself. He thought of the shy Desir and the conversations they had recently enjoyed. What would happen to her now? Would being a barmaid destroy her completely? What else might she be required to do? He put the thought from his mind.

A troop of soldiers trotted by in even, shining ranks. As they swept past, they pushed Joseph tightly against the wall. Their glistening lances seemed to pierce the sky. He crouched there and reviewed again in his mind the journey to Memphis. The blatant market place faded from his senses as his mind went back to their journey.

From the border fortress of Khetem, the caravan dropped out of the harsh desert environment into the verdant green pastures and fields of what Balshazar called Goshen. Goshen was a land of marshes and pastures as far as the eye could see on either side. Joseph thought of the dry, rocky pastures where his father's herds browsed. What a contrast. Wouldn't his father and brothers enjoy pasturing their flocks here! After two weeks of desert his eyes took in everything: marshes where papyrus and rushes grew taller than a man; numberless flocks of ducks and geese and swans in every pond and canal; huge basins and manmade irrigation ditches crisscrossing the flats; wild oxen, antelope, cattle, and sheep. What impressed Joseph most, though, was the greenness.

Balshazar acted excited to be in Egypt. He could hardly sit still on his camel. The trail broadened and paralleled a canal cut through the red earth. Balshazar told Joseph how the canal had been dug by slave labor to join the delta of the Nile with the Red Sea. Joseph pictured in his mind each shovelful of dirt carried by slaves from the huge trench.

He shook his head. "I'm amazed."

Balshazar smiled broadly. "If you are amazed at this, I will show you something in a few days that will astonish you."

Joseph looked curiously at his master.

The trail stretched out beside the canal until it intersected a tributary of the Nile River. Here the trail turned south. Two days after leaving Khetem, they came to the border town of Per Sopt. That night the caravan camped in a grove outside the town. Balshazar set up his trade goods on tables before his tent. Even before it was set up, the camp swarmed with people.

Joseph watched the Egyptians as he recorded transactions. The men, slight of build but broad-shouldered, had high noses and cheekbones. Most had dark hair and eyes and skin of a deep dark brown hue. Women's features were similar but their skin color seemed lighter — more a light, yellowish brown. Both men and women wore white, short-sleeved, lined garments with pleated skirts that hung to the knee.

At noon of the third day after leaving Khetem, they rounded a bank of the river tributary they had followed. Before them lay the magnificent city of On. Balshazar had described this temple city, but his description had not prepared Joseph. His first view of the fabled city almost took his breath away. Never had he seen so many buildings! High above the houses soared roofs and spires of temples and palaces. Golden On, city of the Sun, lay at the apex of the Nile delta. To Joseph's eyes it seemed almost as if the city had been crafted from gold. He sat spellbound, gazing at the wonder of it. His eyes kept returning to the great glittering obelisk before the massive temple.

Akdar shouted. "Come! You hold up the caravan."

Still looking over the panorama of the great city, Joseph clucked to his camel. He hoped to see inside this fabulous city, but Balshazar was impatient to get to Memphis. He mumbled to Joseph that the priests taxed the people of On so heavily for the temples that they had no money to buy his goods. But Memphis, which lay upstream and across the river, was a great merchant city. From the bluff above the city Joseph caught his first look at the great Nile. It was at least a mile across! He had been to the Jordan River several times, but the Jordan was a trickle in the sand compared to the great river before him.

An hour's ride upstream, Balshazar led them to the river bank. A large, flat-bottomed ferry made of palm trunks laced solidly together floated against the dock. An Egyptian in a white robe stood on the dock surveying the work of two glistening, black Nubian slaves.

Balshazar shouted. "Djuh! It has been a long time."

The Egyptian looked up at Balshazar, then glanced at the rest of the caravan. Joseph could almost see the greed in his eyes as he opened his snaggle-toothed mouth. "You want to cross my river?" he asked as he unconsciously rubbed his palms together.

Balshazar stepped off his kneeling camel. With much shouting and arm-waving, the two men haggled.

Joseph, curious as always, sat on the bank and watched the flotilla of boats gliding through the water. Great, brown sails fluttered from tall masts. What amazed Joseph was that boats went in both directions — some upstream and some down. How could a boat go against the current?

Getting camels, asses, and people across the river was an all-afternoon job. The ferryman took only six camels at a time. As his group went across, Joseph delighted in watching the two blacks as they skillfully poled the awkward raft. As they worked their poles, they sang long, monotonous chants. The river water was reddish-brown, the current slow and phlegmatic. Still the raft drifted far downstream before it touched the opposite bank. The Nubian polers had to pole upstream against the current to pick up the next load. They seemed uncomplaining and almost tireless.

Once ashore, Joseph had much time to wait for the rest of the caravan to arrive. He ordered Balshazar's tent set up, then motioned for Desir to come sit with him so they could talk. He really enjoyed these moments when they talked and discussed the meaning of life. It had been difficult for Joseph to cheer Desir. Snatched from those she loved, made a slave, abused by those who captured her, had seriously lowered her self-image.

Flies and gnats buzzed half-heartedly around their heads. Lying on the bank, watching the caravan cross the river, made Joseph very lazy. But he felt a stiffness in Desir. She sat on the clay bank, her back to him, chewing on a twig. He didn't attempt to interrupt her reverie.

Suddenly she turned to him, her eyes flashing. "I wish I were dead."

The suddenness of her statement took him by surprise. He did not know how to respond. He could see the seriousness in her eyes, in the set of her mouth and jaw. He didn't answer her.

She turned quickly away, but not before Joseph saw that her eyes brimmed with tears. He felt so helpless. He tried to think of some empathetic statement like, "I know how you feel." But he really did not know. He might be a slave, but life still meant a great deal to him. He gloried in each day and the adventure of it. Quickly thinking back to when he had felt so sorry for himself in the pit, he asked himself: Did I feel life was not worth living? No. Even then, I wanted to live. He put his hand on her shoulder, amazed at how thin she was. "Desir," he groped for words. "I'm trying to understand how you feel, and I recalled a Sumerian poem my aunt Bilhah used to sing to me. Let me see if I can remember it.

Some people have said the world is a dismal place;
But I know better, for I have seen the dawn,

Walked in the splendor of a morning's sun,
And blinked at the brilliance of the dew.
Some have said the world is sad;
I can't agree, for I have heard the cheerful songs of
Feathered birds; heard the low laughter of the leaves,
And the everlasting chuckle of a mountain brook.
Some have said the world's a musty sordid thing;
It cannot be true, for I have seen the rain –
Watched it bathe the earth, and I have seen the sky,
Newly scrubbed and spotless, blue from end to end.
Some have said the world is evil;
But they are wrong, for I have known its people –
Watched them live, love and labor –
Watched them hope, dream, and pray.
I've heard people say these things; but I would disagree,
For, for every shadow I have seen a hundred rays of light.
For every plaintive note I have heard great songs of joy.
For every mite of bad, I have found a homer of good.

Desir sat silently, her head bowed. Joseph felt a touch on his arm and looked into Desir's reddened eyes. She sniffed and blinked to clear the tears. "Thank you," she whispered as she squeezed his arm. "That was beautiful." She paused, getting control of her emotions. "I will not complain again. Life is worth living."

He pulled her until her head rested on his shoulder. Together, they watched the ships sailing up and down the Nile.

An hour after breaking camp the next morning, the caravan topped a small ridge. Joseph, wide-eyed, pulled his camel to a stop. Before him lay an awesome spectacle – huge triangles of stone, stair-stepping high into the sky. Mountains – but mountains created by the hand of man; in fact, by the hands of many thousands of men. Balshazar reined alongside, a broad grin on his face. He answered Joseph's unasked questions. He told him about the great Pharaohs, of their burial monuments, of the hundreds of thousands of slave days required to build each monument. As the caravan went onward, one after another of the huge, triangular shapes rose from the desert floor. They were objects of splendor ... and death. Joseph involuntarily shuddered.

Balshazar pointed out the huge god-beast lying before the tallest pyramid. He explained that it was Hor-im-akhet, the great Sphinx. The caravan rode right up to its base. Joseph's camel stood by a front paw of the Sphinx: the paw stood taller than a tall house. High above him the head looked eastward with large wide-open eyes. Joseph had never seen anything like it. In fact, if he did not see it now he would not have believed such a thing could exist.

He rode in silence the rest of the way to the city. Nothing he could say could express his feelings of awe. Joseph struggled in his own mind with the feelings of timelessness. *When did it all begin? What is the Lord's scheme of things? When will it end?* The pyramids provided for him a look at the ancient past. He asked himself again, *What will the future hold for me?*

Gates of the city rose before them. The city of Memphis — an ancient city — existed before the pyramids. As they passed through the gates, the bustling life of the city swept Joseph along with it. Never had he been around such great numbers of people. The city seethed with hordes of quarreling and garrulous men. As the caravan clattered through narrow, winding streets, each part of the city seemed to have its own distinct personality. The caravan passed down a broad, tree-lined avenue. Here were huge homes built of stones and whitewashed clay bricks. Gates led from streets to beautiful gardens. From the street Joseph could see tops of shade trees above the roof-line of the houses. His neck became stiff just from gawking at it all.

The market place lay in the center of the city. Located next to it was the caravanserai where they would lodge. Crammed inside the dirty brick courtyard were Nubians, Syrians, desert Arabs, and Libyans. Bleating of animals, squealing and whining of blind beggars, sounds of musical instruments formed a cacophony of sound. Joseph felt pushed and shoved from all sides. Only the heavily laden camels strode calmly, uncaring through the tumult.

Beside gutters, barbers shaved customers, cobblers repaired sandals and harness, potters whirled clay into pots of all sizes and shapes. All seemed bustle and confusion. Shouts of merchants mingled with voices of buyers. Each person seemed to try to shout louder than the next. Joseph felt hemmed in. The sun beat down between the walls, stifling him. He longed for the openness of the desert or the beauty of the hills of home. White dust lay over everything. Strong scent of spices mingled with smells of people and animals and stench of bad fish and overripe fruit. He felt his already limited freedom further eroded. Then he remembered the advice he had given Desir: "You always have the freedom to control your own thoughts. Freedom is within you."

For three days Joseph had no time even to think. From dawn to dark they frequented the crowded and noisy market. Everything was there: strings of onions, melons, little hard figs of the sycamore tree, citrus fruits he had never seen or tasted — oranges, lemons. Peppers, leeks, and cucumbers hung in abundance. Pots of honey, rag-wrapped bundles of raisins, fresh grapes, jars of concoctions without number in all shapes and sizes filled the booths. Heaps of walnuts and almonds and crescent-shaped pancakes stuffed with fillings of all kinds lined the walls. Then there were the exotic items brought by Balshazar's caravan — spices and ointments, trade goods from Syria, frankincense and myrrh. Each night Joseph crawled onto his pallet exhausted just from the sheer crowds and the pressure of recording each transaction.

The cries of the slave auctioneer brought him back to the present. Syrian trade goods and slaves, including Desir, had all been sold. Joseph looked once more over the heads of the crowd, trying to get one last look at Desir. No use. She had disappeared, pulled along by the fat tavern keeper who had purchased her. He returned with the caravaners to the caravanserai and sought out Akdar. "What will happen now?"

Akdar shrugged. "We rest for a few days, then we load the camels with Egyptian gold and linen and return to Gilead."

Balshazar bustled up, rubbing his fat hands with glee. He had made a substantial profit on this caravan. Now they would celebrate. But first there was one more task. He had saved back some of the more expensive perfumes to take to the Pharaoh. That was his insurance to continue his trade in mighty Egypt. While in Avaris, presenting his gift to Pharaoh, he would also sell Joseph to Potiphar. That, too, should be very profitable to him.

"Ho, young Joseph," he grinned. "We prospered in the market place. You brought me such good fortune that I will dislike parting with you." He pursed his lips. His small eyes assumed a greedy look. "But we must go back across the desert and I have no intention of taking you back where your people might give me problems." He nodded at Akdar. "Is all in readiness?"

Akdar nodded.

"Good. We will move camp outside the city while I make arrangements for a river trip to Avaris." Now he was all business. "Akdar, take charge of the camels. Bed them, give them good food and rest. Next week we begin purchasing for our return trip."

Joseph looked at him. "What about me?"

Balshazar smiled. "Tomorrow morning we take ship. You and I will journey downstream to the court of Pharaoh."

"As thou wilt," Joseph meekly replied.

Balshazar, loquacious, continued talking as if he had not heard Joseph. "Pharaoh's court is in the city of Avaris. It is the old Egyptian city of Zoan." He laughed. "When the Hyksos captured Egypt, they needed a capital closer to their own lands. That's why they chose Zoan. Besides, they did not want to have anything to do with Memphis or Thebes where the previous Pharaohs dwelt."

The sun had just started its long journey up the sky when Balshazar and Joseph walked down the dock. Other than the short ferry ride across the river, Joseph had never been on a boat. He gawked at the sight of the huge ship with scrubbed deck and tall mast. He climbed aboard eagerly, curious to explore this new marvel. As soon as they were on board, the Egyptian captain signaled his crew. They cast off mooring ropes and headed north on the dawn-pinkened waters of the Nile.

Now Joseph had time to enjoy sailing. A lookout, stationed on the bow took soundings. Joseph could not understand what he shouted, but as the man stuck the long pole into the water alongside the goose-neck prow, Joseph knew his purpose. Planks creaked, taut ropes sang, and water hissed softly past the hull. The captain sat on the slanting beak in the stern of the ship, operating the long rudder arm. The only clothing he and the other deeply-browned crew members wore were loincloths which Joseph learned were called shentis. The ship carried cargo for Avaris: bales of linen, papyrus, rope, sacks of lentils, and several other passengers.

Joseph spread his mat on the rolling deck and lay on his back watching the mast trace great circles against the brilliant sky. The great rudder sweep screeched rhythmically in its socket. High overhead, where the sweep's tall shaft met the top of the rudder post, lashings creaked in echo as they rubbed across the cow's horn which supported them.

By late afternoon they left the main channel, turning right into one of the Nile's many sluggish branches. As the sun set, the ship glided under oars into the docking area of Bubastis, and soon swayed at its hawser as the current gently lifted it and let it fall. The sailors, seeking wine and excitement secured the ship and quietly left. Joseph and Balshazar stayed on board.

Joseph lay on his mat, deep in thought, watching the mast that seemed to rotate around several heavenly constellations. Sleep came quickly to the tired youth. As he slept he dreamed of a slavemaster, all dressed in white linen. He seemed to be running alongside the huge, brown river with the slavemaster fast on his heels. A slavemaster who was captain of the guard, chief executioner of Pharaoh — whose name was Potiphar.

Chapter 6: In Potiphar's Service

Joseph scrubbed his arms and hands, thinking *I wonder how many times I have washed myself in the eleven months since I have been at Potiphar's estate.* He smiled. *I have washed here more in one month than in my entire seventeen years in Haran and Canaan.*

Not that I mind, he reflected, holding his arms over the bowl so that Amet could pour rinse water over them. *Being clean is like having your head shaved – once you get used to the feel of it you rather like it. I also enjoy wearing the thin linen shentis. It is much nicer than the rough Canaanite cloth. I like the cool and pleasantly crisp feel against my thighs. I feel better clean – and I know I smell better.* He raised a wrist to his nose. *I smell like an Egyptian,* he thought. Smiling, he remembered the half-alien, half-familiar mingling of scents which had risen from Potiphar's courtyard the day Balshazar brought him here to be sold to Potiphar.

His first view of Potiphar's estate had been the covered gate opening to the courtyard. The shady court faced an open, double gate flanked by stately palm trees. Standing in the square, inner court, Joseph could see the large house in the center of the grounds, surrounded on the west and south by spacious green gardens. Other buildings lined walls to the north and east.

Balshazar spoke with Potiphar's overseer, an older, stocky, strongly-built man. He was clean-shaven with a full head of black hair streaked with gray. His eyes had a kindly glint. Joseph knew at once he would like this man. "Ah, Nefertekh," Balshazar said expansively. "Look what I have brought you from the east."

Nefertekh, the overseer, looked at him suspiciously. "The last time you brought me rotten fruit and shoddy merchandise."

Smiling, Balshazar bowed. "Ah, my friend. You belittle the treasures I have bestowed on you. But this time ..." he swept his arm out to indicate Joseph. " ... we heard you seek a good servant. I have brought a servant that will please you."

The overseer inspected Joseph as he would a fine horse. He pinched him in the back, ran his fingers through his hair, looked into his eyes. Joseph, humiliated, stood without talking. Seeming satisfied, Nefertekh asked, "Why do you feel another slave will please my master?"

"Oh, this is not just another slave," extolled Balshazar. "This slave is not only skilled in reading and writing but has dexterity with numbers and accounts."

Joseph stood mutely before the overseer.

"What is he worth?" Nefertekh growled.

"At least four hundred debens of copper," Balshazar rolled his eyes towards the heavens.

Nefertekh laughed. "Four hundred? I can buy five good slaves for four hundred. Because he can keep accounts I will give you one hundred debens."

Sadly and dramatically, Balshazar shook his head. "No. I could have gotten that at the slave auction. It would be a sacrifice to let him go for three hundred debens."

Nefertekh walked around Joseph again. The bargaining process was slow. "My master is a tough trader. I will give you two hundred debens, but only if you bring me fresh onions and wine when you return from the lands to the north."

Balshazar smiled. He had satisfied his mercantile conscience by getting a good price for his young slave. He put his hand on Joseph's arm. "My son, I would gladly have kept you to keep my own accounts. However, farewell. Show yourself worthy of being owned by Potiphar. He will be a kindly master."

Balshazar accepted the bag of coins from Nefertekh and went across the court and through the gateway. Joseph looked after him, a hollow feeling in the pit of his stomach. *What will happen now?*

He did not have long to wonder. Nefertekh grabbed him and hustled him toward a low, barracks-like building. The building housed slaves and servants. Servants bathed him, shaved him bald, gave him fresh clothes, and hung a gold medallion around his neck.

From the first day Nefertekh took advantage of Joseph's skill in reading and writing. He put him to work as his personal assistant. Joseph spent most of his days writing up the numerous accounts of his master. To be cooped up inside depressed him. Often Joseph looked longingly beyond the high walls at palms which waved heavy heads against the brilliant sky.

Weeks went by as Joseph learned the estate record-keeping system. He made lists, kept accounts, and learned Egyptian. Soon he handled all the accounts of the vast estate. In addition to being one of Pharaoh's chief officers, Potiphar had developed his estate into a large business operation. His estate yielded farm produce and a variety of manufactured goods. As he handled the accounts, Joseph realized Potiphar was a very wealthy man.

Joseph had a continuing hunger for new learning. As he ate meals with the servants in the servants' house, he listened carefully, filing in his memory information he thought he might be able to use. His Egyptian, quaint and stilted when he arrived on the estate, became flawless. He listened to accents of language and to rumors and gossip. He became skillful at imitating servants' idioms and soon could chatter with the best of them.

Joseph sighed. *I cannot dwell on my memories.* Amet had finished washing him. He was ready to go to the school of the scribes. *I am thankful Nefertekh prescribed scribe training for me. Without that break from the monotony of the estate — ?* He left the thought dangling. He turned back to the barracks, knotted a clean linen shentis around his lean hips, bound on a plain headcloth, groped in the gloom for his sandals, then stepped out into the sun's bright glare.

Later that morning, just like every morning at the school of the scribes, Joseph sat cross-legged on a woven mat. He set out his writing materials: a vial of water, a rectangular pallet — slotted to hold his reed pens and hollowed for two of the ink cakes — and a smooth, plastered writing board which could be washed clean at the end of each lesson. Each day he noticed improvement in his writing and in his understanding of Egyptian picture writing.

After his lesson he returned to the villa. From the direction of the Nile he heard shouting of rivermen and slapping of sails. *If only* — he thought. He sighed. *To have been purchased — much like a sheep or a camel — still depresses me. I hate to think of myself as a piece of merchandise.* He analyzed his service thus far in Egypt. *My life has not been perfect, but I feel I have lived in accordance with God's will — as far as I know His will.* He shook his head. Life at Potiphar's estate does not lend itself well to a spiritual life. I have no privacy. Someone regulates and prescribes every minute of every day. From the moment I wake in the barracks to the moment I return at night, there is someone telling me what to do.

One evening Nefertekh called him from his records. "Bathe and put on a clean robe."

Joseph bowed, not daring to ask the purpose of cleaning up.

"You are to serve Potiphar at dinner."

"But I . . ."

"Never mind. Just get ready. I will show you what to do."

Nefertekh, with Joseph beside him, stood behind Potiphar's chair.

Joseph spent much of his time observing his master. Potiphar was heavy-set and beardless. Always before when Joseph had seen him, Potiphar had worn a wig. Now he saw that his master was bald. Long lashes veiled black and piercing eyes. An aristocratic, hooked nose dominated his face. He had a prominent chin and a small mouth which often had a pleasant smile.

Potiphar's chief wife, Zelicah, much younger than Potiphar, looked lovely in a beautiful, transparent dress. A heavy gold collar girdled her throat. She chattered gaily with Potiphar and other guests, paying little attention to the tall slave behind her husband's chair. Once she did look at him, with the faintest shadow of a smile showing in her enamel-lengthened eyes and in the corners of her sensuous mouth.

Family members and guests showed respect and consideration for each other. Their dignity and self-confidence impressed Joseph. He made a mental note to model his behavior after what he observed.

As green fields turned golden and ready for harvest, Joseph found himself taking over more and more of Nefertekh's duties around the estate. He rationed out provisions to workers and servants, ordered bread, beer, and barley; supplied the women's house with needed supplies; ordered raw materials for the bakers, sandal makers, brewers, weavers, and spinners, then arranged to have their finished wares sold. He supervised the harvest and storage or marketing of the wheat and fruits. Even the estate's livestock came under his jurisdiction: horses that drew Potiphar's chariot, his dogs, and the herd of fine cattle pastured on part of the estate. Potiphar's vast fields consisted of five hundred square rods of farmland and about the same amount of pasture.

As time went on, Joseph accompanied Nefertekh on business trips into On and Memphis. Soon, however, Nefertekh sent Joseph on errands by himself. Joseph became master of the bark, taking Potiphar's goods to market and bringing back trade goods for the estate.

Some servants resented him, not only because he was a Semite and a slave, but because Nefertekh showed such favoritism to him. Hearing of these jealousies, Joseph shrugged and continued his work. One, especially cool to Joseph, was Beku, keeper of the orchard. Joseph tried his best to be friendly to Beku, but it did no good. Beku constantly stirred up trouble between Joseph and the other workers.

Nefertekh moved Joseph from the slave quarters to the main house. His room, under a stairway leading upstairs in the large home, was tiny, but comfortable. Joseph's furniture consisted of a bedstead covered with leopard skin and with great elephant feet carved legs. There was a chest for his very own use and a stand and stone washbowl. No window opened in Joseph's room, and it remained dark and cool even in midday. To walk out of the sun into his room pleasantly sliced burning heat off his shoulders as if by a cool knife blade.

Five years passed. Potiphar called the young Joseph to his study. The room, filled with chests and shelves, statuettes in silver and gold, ivory and ebony, impressed the slave, Joseph. Crowns and headdresses adorned the shelves. Handsomely decorated bookcases, filled with elegantly carved handles holding roll after roll of papyrus, lined one wall. Joseph had never seen a library before.

Potiphar looked up from his desk where he had a papyrus roll spread open before him. For several moments he held Joseph's blue eyes with his own as the young man stood before him. Finally he spoke: "I have observed your work around the estate. Nefertekh tells me you are his right hand." Joseph bowed respectfully.

"You are a slave?"

Joseph nodded.

"How long have you worked here at my estate?"

"Five years, master."

"What tasks have been your responsibilities?"

Joseph enumerated them on his fingers. "I have kept my master's accounts; have purchased supplies for the servants' quarters and the main house; have sold my master's produce at the market place; and have also sold my master's trade goods at the market."

Potiphar nodded. "Nefertekh said you are a sharp trader — that you have increased my wealth manyfold through your trading."

Joseph lowered his eyes respectfully.

Potiphar stood and walked to the bookcase, replacing the papyrus roll. Turning, he stated, "Nefertekh is ill. He requested he be granted leave from his duties. He recommended you replace him as overseer."

Joseph stood speechless before Potiphar. Nefertekh ill! Overseer of the vast estate of Potiphar? So that is why Nefertekh delegated so many responsibilities to me. Then showing his concern, he asked, "Great master, may I ask what troubles Nefertekh?"

Potiphar shrugged. "The physician is not sure. He feels there is not much time." He added sadly, as if to himself, "Nefertekh served me faithfully for over twenty years. I am willing to accept his recommendation that you serve in his place."

Joseph bowed again. "I will do your will, great master."

Potiphar put a hand on Joseph's shoulder and guided him through the door. They walked into the bright sunlight together, past the sundial in the open court, past the house of women, the cook house, and the house of the servants. Potiphar stopped in a kiosk near the orchard. He motioned Joseph to a seat on the bench which ringed the small building. From where they sat they could look out past the orchard with its green foliage to the vineyards and finally to the flat, open fields.

Sweeping his arm to encompass all they could see, Potiphar spoke. "This will be yours to govern. I keep busy with my duties at the palace." He turned to Joseph and spoke kindly. "You are not an Egyptian. From where did you come?"

Joseph explained about his land and his people. As he talked of his father, he again felt that strong bond, as if his father still lived and God wanted him to know it.

"Your people are important to you." It was a statement, not a question.

Joseph had a feeling that Potiphar tested him. Many times Nefertekh had philosophized with him. Was Potiphar doing that now? He looked at his kindly master. "There is not a day goes by that I do not think of my family. There is an old Hebrew saying I learned as a child: Before you know who you are and where you are going you must know from whence you came."

Potiphar spoke. "Heritage is important. Without heritage we are drifters. He sat silently, looking over his fields." He continued. "Nefertekh feels you are very capable. That is still to be fully proven. With so many decisions to be made, you are bound to make mistakes. Are you willing to do that?"

Looking at Potiphar intently to catch his meaning, Joseph nodded. "My lord, I feel to stumble is part of growing. I have found in my own life that it takes faith to get up after you have fallen or been knocked down." He paused, then said quietly. "I have that faith."

Potiphar seemed pleased with Joseph's answer. He rose. "I must be going. Joseph, I am trusting my entire estate to you."

Joseph dropped to his knees before Potiphar. "I will not betray your trust."

Joseph, almost twenty-four, was no longer a youth. His body had filled out broad and firm. His face was full and more serious, his features regular and refined. Externally, Joseph looked like an Egyptian. He spoke the Egyptian language fluently. His clean-shaven face had darkened from exposure to the sun. He dressed in Egyptian linen — a short-sleeved tunic, a pleated skirt, laced sandals. Around his neck he wore a gold chain with a scarab amulet. A second but plain amulet also hung from his neck. It was a small leather bag with a drawstring at the top. It only contained one thing: a small, smooth, green-colored rock.

Sometimes, Joseph felt as if he lived two lives — never forgetting his heritage, but accepting and adopting that part of the Egyptian culture which fit his needs. Coming to Egypt when still young and pliable, Joseph realized it had been easy for him to adjust. Though I am a subject of Pharaoh, and a slave of Potiphar, I am fiercely loyal to the One God who brought me into this land. This is not a bad life. I live better than most free Egyptians. He often wondered what had happened to Desir. How has she changed? He had thought several times he would like to be married, but had put that from his mind. I am a slave, and slaves do not marry.

Stepping out of the brewery shed one afternoon, he saw a girl walking toward the main house. He recognized her as Asenath, the twelve-year-old daughter of Potiphar's second wife, Khenwet. She was tall and slender, with all the charm of her tender years. Her hair, black and very long, hung below her waist. He had only seen Asenath a few times because she and her mother isolated themselves in the women's section. He watched as she walked back to her quarters. She moved with a flowing and natural grace. As she entered the door, she turned, giving Joseph a long look out of large, dark eyes.

Something troubled him. For a moment he had a feeling of . . . but no, he threw off the feeling. A slave cannot think of the daughter of an officer of Pharaoh. He put the thought from his mind, but that night, as he lay in bed, those eyes continued to haunt him. I have not had much time to think about women, he thought as he lay there. Running this huge estate keeps me busy from morning until night. My head is too full of figures, facts, and all sorts of detail to think of personal pleasure. Besides, I am still not sure of God's purpose for me. I must be totally devoted to duty in order to fulfill that purpose. Potiphar trusts me with everything on the estate. I feel it important to live up to that trust.

One night, especially tired and frustrated, he sat by Nefertekh's bedside. For a while he just sat there as the old man slept. Finally, Nefertekh opened glazed eyes. He squinted, not seeming to realize who sat by him. When he did, his hand moved over and weakly grasped Joseph's hand.

"What is it, my friend?"

"My responsibilities seem so overpowering at times. There are so many things to do. It seems I run constantly but never get through."

Nefertekh squeezed Joseph's hand. "I understand," he whispered. After a moment he asked, "Joseph, have you seen the pyramids?"

Joseph nodded.

"To look at the whole project of building a pyramid would be overwhelming, but remember those who built the pyramids laid up just one stone at a time."

"That is a good analogy, but . . ."

Nefertekh interrupted. "Some people never try because they fear they won't be successful. It is better to try and fail than to be a failure by never trying."

Joseph leaned forward and studied the sagging face of his friend and former master. "Thank you for your words of encouragement."

Eyes closed, Nefertekh squeezed Joseph's hand, then his grip relaxed as sleep overcame him.

Chapter 7: Zelicah

Joseph often supervised serving dinner. Potiphar's family became a proxy family to him — a feeling of the family he no longer had. The family ate in the dining hall, a high-ceilinged and bright room. Light came from open windows and doors. The light-blue, painted ceiling contrasted with white crossbeams supported by blue wooden columns. Serving tables and lamps lined the walls.

One morning Potiphar called Joseph. "Dinner will be extra special this evening. Pharaoh's assistant, the vizier, will visit our estate." Joseph organized dinner with his usual eye for details. Servants scrubbed down the dinner hall and spread fresh rushes on the floor. They shined the table to a bright luster. Attendants and servers, dressed in clean linen, stood ready to serve the meal.

The kitchen prepared main courses of roast duck and goose, joints of beef, and fish. Side dishes of fresh vegetables, melons, and fruits from the estate, and steaming loaves of hot bread and cakes heaped high on the serving tables completed the meal.

The family and royal guest entered the room, sat down, and waited to be served. Servants scurried to and fro on bare feet to serve the various courses. Joseph, dressed in his very finest, stood behind Potiphar's chair directing his staff. He wore a head cloth of ribbed black silk, an enameled collar, arm bands, with a knee-length double skirt around his narrow hips. The sheer white of his skirt set off the warm bronze-tone of his flesh. He stood, his youthful body perfect and strong. His eyes, friendly and expressive, shone from his face.

Family and guest conversed infrequently and in soft voices. Zelicah, Potiphar's chief wife, dressed elegantly in a pure white robe trimmed with beautiful embroidery in bright colors. A wide gold collar banded her neck. Her eyes, painted and enamel-lengthened, roved from person to person. When Joseph handed a dish to his master, or filled his cup, her eyes often rested upon him. Whenever her eyes met his, he quickly looked away. Eye contact with the master's wife did not seem fitting.

Joseph had seen his mistress, Zelicah, few times. Occasionally, as she swayed past in her carrying chair, he had caught brief glimpses of her. Her wig of bright blue hung far down onto her shoulders. As chief wife of Potiphar, she had every luxury. Servants and slaves waited her constant call. The first and titular wife, she dominated all other females in Potiphar's harem. She hosted at all functions as female head of the estate. Now her eyes lingered on Joseph. He felt very uncomfortable under her gaze.

As days passed, Joseph seemed to bump into Zelicah everywhere he went. Whether he supervised slaves and servants in his master's house, or managed the vast agricultural ventures, or supervised the shops, Zelicah found him. Alarmed, he tried to avoid her as he made his rounds on the estate. He desired to act with good sense and propriety, but he did not count on Zelicah's ardor. He went to visit Nefertekh. For a few moments they discussed the estate — the endless details needing the attention of the overseer. Joseph felt dismayed to see his friend so haggard. The strong body had been reduced to a shadow of its once formidable self.

Nefertekh, pale and wan, apparently had little strength, but he smiled. "Come now, my friend. You did not come to discuss the estate. You have handled that well for years. What troubles you?"

Joseph sighed. He did not know how to handle the delicate situation. "It's the mistress, Zelicah." He paused, not sure whether to express his suspicions. "She seems to have taken an interest in me. I am not sure what to do."

Nefertekh stared at the ceiling. "Hmmm. That is a problem for one in your position. Does Potiphar suspect what is happening?"

"I don't know. I have done nothing that would give cause for suspicion." Nefertekh nodded. "I know, but have you done anything to encourage Zelicah."

"Nothing."

"Then there is nothing you can do but try to avoid her."

"Should I go to Potiphar?"

"No. That would not be appropriate."

"I cannot believe God would bring me to Egypt only to let me fall before the wiles of this woman."

"I don't know your God, Joseph, but I believe God does not make mistakes. Trust in him."

"Thanks. You are a source of strength and comfort to me." Joseph squeezed Nefertekh's thin shoulder, then left. In his room, he dropped to his knees on the clay floor and poured out his heart to God.

The next day Zelicah asked him to meet her in the kiosk. Joseph took a roll of accounts with him, wanting to have something to work on. As he strode toward the kiosk, he passed the servant, Beku, who looked at him with loathing.

Fluted columns and floral garlands decorated the open kiosk. A long, elegant couch of ebony and ivory — spread with panther and lynx skins and strewn with soft cushions — lined its interior. Zelicah lay on the couch. A Nubian girl sat at her feet, strumming soft-stringed music. At Joseph's approach, Zelicah raised up on one elbow. She wore a white mantle which fitted her closely and gave majesty to her figure. A golden headcloth framed her delicate features. Painted, jewel-like eyes showed clearly from the shadows. She beckoned Joseph closer.

Reluctantly, he stepped forward, then turned to the roll in his hands. His voice was kind but firm. "My mistress, did you want to look at my accounts?"

She took his hand and pulled him toward the couch. "No, handsome one, I want to look at you. Your appearance and form are magnificent. I have looked at all the slaves and have never seen so beautiful a slave as you."

Joseph stiffened, trying to pull his hand from hers.

"Your eyes are also beautiful," she teased, knowing she made him uncomfortable. "Have they dazzled all the inhabitants of Egypt?" A tantalizing smiled played on her lips. Her eyes reminded Joseph of a cat's, dark and unreadable. She attempted to pull him down to the couch beside her. Joseph stood firm, but she still held his hand. "Joseph, take the harp and play me a song."

He shook his head. "The only songs I know are songs of praise to my God." Joseph knew he must get away. "My mistress," he said, "please. I must attend to your husband's duties."

Ignoring the young female slave, Zelicah made one more attempt. "There is no one here but you and me. You may attend to my needs."

Wrenching his hand away, Joseph stepped back, his eyes on the ground. "My lady, it is necessary that I go." He turned and stumbled out of the kiosk, feeling Zelicah's eyes burning into his back. A cold sweat dampened his face. *What am I to do?*

Joseph's life became miserable. Only Nefertekh's words and his prayers to the One God consoled him. He concentrated fully on managing Potiphar's affairs. Almost daily, Zelicah confronted him on some pretext or other. One day while balancing the account of the weavers, Zelicah came in. She sat on the bench beside him. He could smell her heady perfume, could feel the warmth and closeness of her body revealed by the filmy and almost transparent linen gown. He turned from her, trying to concentrate on the figures before him.

She ran her fingers through his hair, stroking his neck. He shuddered. "What is it, my Joseph?" she asked, her voice low and sultry.

"Please," he said. "Will you not just leave me to my work?"

"Is it that you do not think me beautiful?"

"You are very beautiful."

"Then why will you not lie with me?"

Joseph blushed. He tried to explain his vow to the Lord, but the idea seemed too complicated to Zelicah. In a land where gods smiled on all relationships between men and women, she seemed unable to comprehend a God who would forbid such relationships.

Zelicah became angry. "If you will not do what I ask, I will have an iron yoke put upon you and have you thrown into the dungeon."

Dealing with her anger was easier than dealing with her flirtation. He faced her for the first time. "Do with me what you will, but I will not lie with you. God himself will release me from your fetters."

She shouted. "You shall have a slow, lingering death. I will have them hang you upside down till the blood rushes to your head and death finally comes."

Shaking his head, Joseph attempted to push past her to the door. She completely lost her self-control, became irrational with emotion. "I shall have you fed to the crocodiles. You shall be tied and left in the reeds of the Nile for the crocodiles to feed on."

"My mistress, no matter what you might do to me, I cannot give in to your desire. I have given a promise to God. If I broke that promise he would destroy me."

She turned and stalked from the room.

Joseph breathed a sigh of relief.

To celebrate her birthday, Zelicah invited a great many ladies to the estate for a luncheon. She assigned Joseph as the main steward for the afternoon affair. Fragrant flowers lined the walls of the great hall. Cool, refreshing wines flowed freely as the ladies socialized. Refreshments: cakes, fruits, sweetmeats filled tables. Potiphar employed a flutist and harpist to provide music.

The ladies sat on benches visiting until time for the meal to be served. Zelicah clapped her hands to summon the servants to bring the food. As they ate, she clapped again. Joseph, draped in an elegant linen robe, came in with a pitcher to pour drinks. A stillness settled over the ladies who cast delighted glances at the handsome and embarrassed Joseph.

Semekh said, "That slave of yours is a beauty. I cannot keep my eyes off him."

Zelicah said, "You observed his beauty in the few moments he has been before you. How do you think I feel when he is always in my house? I see him day after day."

One of the ladies asked, "Why not tell him how you feel?"

"I have tried daily to persuade him" Zelicah replied, "but he will not consent to my wishes. I promised him everything, yet he does not come to me."

"Perhaps you could entice him and seize him in secret. Perhaps then he will hearken to you."

The next day Joseph was at work in the den. Zelicah came in silently and put her arms around his neck.

Joseph grabbed her by the wrists and twisted away.

She sank to the ground weeping. "Joseph, my love," she sobbed. "Please listen to me. Have you ever had a woman speak to you as I have and still not respond? Is it because you fear Potiphar? As Pharaoh lives, no harm will come to you because of this. Please, Joseph. Come to me." Joseph shook his head sadly. "No, my lady. This thing I cannot do. The master trusts me with all he possesses. How could I violate that trust?"

He helped her to her feet and walked her to the door. Her head hung and she walked away, as if broken and discouraged. Joseph knew she felt hurt that he did not seem to understand that she had offered him her feelings. But he understood only too well. He also knew the problem had not ended — Zelicah would not give up.

Spring came again. The Nile began its annual flooding, an occasion observed as the official new year in Egypt. Pharaoh called for a festival, the grandest of the entire year. He invited everyone, and expected all to attend — even the slaves. With exception of Zelicah and several of her maids, everyone from the estate went to the festival. Pleading illness, she asked to remain home. Potiphar, seeing her painted paleness, reluctantly consented.

Potiphar drove his magnificent chariot, pulled by his matched team of black chargers. Joseph walked beside Potiphar's carriage, admiring the horses. He had always desired to own horses of his own, but as a slave...

Throughout the city gay flags fluttered from gilded poles. Tables heaped with flowers and fruits lined the shrines of the various gods. The nobility paraded through city streets. Citizens sang and clapped. In the temples, clouds of incense rose to the ceilings, escaping through high windows. Sacred chants mingled with beat of drums and rattle of tambourines. Sweating throngs leaped and danced in exuberance.

Joseph returned early to the estate. There was much work to do. The week's records had not been entered in the books. The sun, shining across the desert, made his office uncomfortably hot. He stripped off his robe. Dressed only in his shentis, he sat at the desk and started to make his entries. A knock came at the door. Joseph, startled, called, "What is it?"

One of Zelicah's Nubian maids, her hair fuzzy and with huge copper disks dangling from her ears, stepped inside. Shyly she handed Joseph a note of papyrus, then slipped out the door.

Joseph opened the scented note. "I have been home ill all day. I am lonesome. I order you to attend me. Zelicah." Crumpling the paper in his hand, he turned back to his desk. *Now what do I do? How can I avoid obeying Zelicah?* He threw his robe over his shoulders and picked up his account books. *Maybe if I enter loaded down with his account books, and begin at once to speak to her about matters of the estate – what can she do?* He knelt in prayer. "Father, I know not what to do. I am strong in my resolve. I am loyal to You, but I feel I need Your strength."

The house of women faced the desert. Bright sun painted black shadows behind each pillar. Joseph had been there several times before, and could picture the room in his mind. He breathed deeply, then crossed the threshold. The room was cool and dim with a heady smell of flowers. Zelicah had prepared well: fingernails and toenails freshly painted, long black hair freshly brushed; her naturally beautiful eyes looked unnaturally large and bright with black antimony applied to brows and lashes; rouge brightened her cheeks; lips were full and sensuous. Her gown, the thinnest of royal linen, revealed more than it covered.

Joseph's self-control faltered at sight of her. He was aroused in spite of himself. He blushed, the red starting at the base of his neck and moving up to his hair line. He shut his eyes and forced his thoughts back to his youth. He pictured himself on his father's knee, listening as Jacob counseled him: "Remember son, your body is a temple of God. Never violate the sacredness of it."

Zelicah took his hand and pulled him into the room. She stroked his arm and looked up into his face. Her breath smelled of incense and honey. From her hair came a fragrance of fine perfume. "Our lives could have been so good if you had accepted me when I first asked you."

"It was impossible then to yield to your request. It is still impossible."

Tears came to her eyes. "I have reduced myself to begging you to fulfill my wishes. I have lost my dignity. Please make me beg no more."

"I am very sorry, my mistress, but you are wife to Potiphar. He placed everything on this estate in my care and trusted me with it. Everything but you. I will not and cannot betray his trust."

She continued to stroke his arm, running her fingers gently along the muscles. "You have great advantages on the estate. If you will but do what I request of you, your advantages will be even greater."

Joseph did not know what else to say. He had given her all of his arguments. He turned to go.

Zelicah grabbed his arm and turned him around. "If you refuse me now, I will tell my husband that you forced yourself upon me."

Joseph shrugged tiredly. "Do what you will."

"He will believe me!" she shouted.

Again he turned to go.

"No!" she shouted with passion. "You cannot leave me. Stay here and love me." She grabbed him again.

Joseph pulled her along as he started out the door. Zelicah held to his robe. Joseph twisted out of it and darted out the door.

She shouted after him. "Stay. Come back!" When he didn't turn, her voice changed to a scream. "Help. Help. The slave, Joseph, tried to defile me." Only her maids heard her.

Wearing only his shentis, Joseph sprinted across the courtyard and into his room. Inside, he shut the door and stood there shaking.

Zelicah, frightened, hurried back to her room, took off her fine linen robe, and put on the plain robe she had worn in her illness. She scrubbed off her makeup, tousled her hair, whitened her face, and went to where she had sat when Potiphar left for the celebration. She put on a look of sadness and waited.

Shadows of evening lengthened by the time Potiphar returned. He wheeled the chariot into the courtyard. A slave took the reins and walked the horses to the stable. Potiphar strode toward the house, pleased with his accomplishments of the day. He drew up short as he saw his wife sprawled on the steps, clutching a tightly-rolled robe in her hands.

"Oh, I am so glad you are home," she cried.

Potiphar noticed how pale and upset she looked. "What troubles you, my dear. Are you still ill?"

She threw her arms around him and clung tightly to him. "The Hebrew slave, Joseph, tried to force me to lie with him." She shuddered dramatically. "He came into my quarters and caught hold of me. But when I screamed he feared for his life and ran, leaving his robe." She buried her face in his shoulder, weeping loudly.

He tried to comfort her, but she pulled away, eyes burning with frustration and anger. "Why did you bring that Hebrew to our house? He has looked upon me with lustful eyes since he first came here." Distraught, Potiphar looked around and spied the slave, Beku. "Fetch Joseph. Bring him to the dining hall."

Walking into the house, Potiphar held his sobbing wife tightly to him. He turned her over to one of her maids, then eased himself into his chair of judgment. His mind was troubled. He loved Joseph like his own son. Perhaps he should not have given Joseph so much trust. Had Joseph become complacent and proud?

His wife's strident voice roused him from his thoughts. "Throw him out of the house. Feed him to the crocodiles. Do what you like with him, but I never want to see his face again."

Potiphar wondered. Zelicah seemed overly dramatic He sorrowed, overcome with disappointment. What can I do? The way was clear before him. The penalty for such action as Joseph was accused of was clearly death.

Joseph shrugged off the hands of a smirking Beku. He entered the great hall, his head held high, his posture erect. Before Potiphar, he bowed and dropped to one knee.

Potiphar looked at him, then shook his head sadly. "Zelicah has witnessed against you. Her word by itself would call for judgment. There is also the evidence of your robe to shame you. What do you say in your defense?"

Joseph remained silent. *What good would it do to speak? My word against that of the mistress?*

"I cannot believe you would do this to me." Potiphar shook his head sadly. "I trusted you with everything I own. You have abused the only thing with which I did not trust you. Have you nothing to say?"

Out of the corner of his eye, Joseph saw the mass of servants and slaves piled into the doorway. Some seemed shocked. Others, like Beku, seemed happy for his predicament. One face caught his attention — the sweet, innocent, wide-eyed face of Asenath.

"My lord," Joseph finally responded, "I have been your loyal slave for ten years. In that time have I ever done any iniquity to you or your household?"

Potiphar shook his head and sighed. "Joseph, ever since you joined my household I have had good luck and prosperity. You have looked after my household as if it were your own. You have increased my wealth and treated my servants fairly. That is what makes this so difficult. My fortunes have multiplied under your leadership. Up to this time you have been a faithful and diligent servant." He paused, deep in thought. He shook his head sadly. "I could have you killed for what has happened here. I cannot bring the judgment of death against you. I therefore sentence you to prison. No more will you belong to me, but to Pharaoh, for you shall be in his prison."

Joseph knew he should be grateful to Potiphar for not having him killed. But prison? A slave of Pharaoh? His legs felt weak. He almost fell, but forced himself to stand upright before his master. Silently he said, *Your will be done, my God. I do not know your purposes, but I must trust in you.*

Chapter 8: Prison Walls

The ship's bow, slapping against the water, sang a monotonous song to Joseph. It seemed to say, "Why? Why?" He lay on a pile of rope, feeling morose and abandoned. *I wonder what could possibly happen next to me. Yes, why?* he thought. He shook his head. *I was heir to my father's inheritance. Instead of receiving it I was cast into a pit, then sold into slavery. I served Potiphar honorably and well, yet now I have been committed to a lifetime in prison. I do not understand.*

He looked at the cloudless sky and whispered aloud, "Why, Lord? How could You let this happen? If I had remained as a servant of Potiphar I could have served You better. What purpose does it serve for me to be in prison?" As soon as he said the words, he felt shamed and bowed his head.

He seemed to hear his father's voice. He pictured again sitting on his father's knee as Jacob told of his father, Isaac being taken to the mountain by his father, Abraham. Abraham had been commanded to sacrifice Isaac. He must have asked, "Why, Lord? He is my only son, my heir. Why must he die?" But the Lord needed to prove Abraham's willingness to sacrifice — his willingness to be obedient — no matter how painful the obedience.

An assurance came to him — a calmness. The Lord will provide — just as he provided the ram for Isaac. He shook his head. That is a great lesson for me. I must learn to trust the Lord amid any perplexing trial for which there is no easy explanation. My own cries of "why" cannot match those of Abraham. But I can utter the same submissive word, "nevertheless." He looked again at the sky and whispered aloud, "I'm sorry Lord. I know You have asked me to just trust You. Please forgive my doubts. I will trust You and continue to serve wherever I am sent."

Hemp cord pinned his hands loosely behind him. He stood and moved around the ship for exercise. Taking short steps to keep his balance on the rolling deck, he strolled back and forth. Red bougainvillea, hibiscus, and oleander lined the riverbanks. Tantalizing, flowery scents drifted across the water. Jacaranda trees trailed lavender lace over the flowers. Joseph sighed. It is a beautiful day, regardless of my destination.

On the shores, peasants harvested crops. The flooding river would soon drive them out, then they would wait for a new planting season in fresh mud. Joseph thought about the parallel of that cycle with his life. I was flooded with love, kindness, and respect, then a drought wiped out everything. I must wait again for the flood. "Lord, I am like a seed of corn," he whispered. "You are planting me again in the mud. I wonder what the harvest will be."

He looked down at himself. His body, tanned dark by the Egyptian sun, was dirty. Gone were his robe, his fine linen, the enameled collar, the armbands, and the golden necklace. There was only one ornament left. He still had the small leather bag with the smooth stone Benjamin had given him. He smiled to himself. I sail up the river just as I sailed down with Balshazar ten years before. But the Joseph who sails upriver toward prison is a far different person than the Joseph Balshazar led to Potiphar's house — though the only things I still own is the loincloth I wear and my Benjamin stone.

"Could I have handled the situation with Zelicah differently?" he asked himself aloud. "Did I, in any way, encourage her flirtation? Should I have informed Potiphar what was happening? Should I have defended myself before Potiphar?" His thoughts tumbled upon themselves. Teeth gritted, he forced negative thoughts from him. *I cannot afford to think about what has been lost. Obviously the Lord has some other mission for me. There must be much yet to be gained.*

He walked the deck immersed in thought. This time on board ship, he had time for introspection and renewed commitment. *What will the Lord want me to do in prison?* Again his own words came to him: *I will serve in whatever position I am placed. I will keep the promise I made to the Lord while in the pit.* After reaffirming that decision he felt relieved. As the ship rounded a bend in the broad river, an island lay before them. On it stood a group of gloomy, brown, sun-dried brick buildings. He had heard the sailors talking of the king's prison, Zawi-Re. Now he viewed it firsthand. The boat pulled up to the dock. Looking curiously at the prison, Joseph made out unpretentious buildings which looked like they could be barracks, storehouses, and workhouses. A smoke cloud rose from the compound.

A motley group of men waited to welcome the ship. Most stood bare-headed and naked except for a shentis. Several guards stood on the dock. Joseph looked at them curiously. Each wore a pleated skirt that hung diagonally to the hollow of the knee. A cuirass of mailed armor covered chests and backs. A snowy-white, short-sleeved linen shirt showed beneath cuirasses. Light brown wigs covered shorn heads, cut straight on the forehead and down to the ears on each side.

One man, in front of the group, stood out. He wore a fine linen head-cloth and a colored robe. Heavy-set, he stood with legs set apart which gave similar appearance to pillars standing mightily before the temple. The man wore neither wig nor cuirass. A dagger hung from his belt. Joseph knew this must be the keeper of the prison. Before he had left Potiphar's estate, the ailing Nefertekh sent word that the prison governor was a friend and would be fair.

The ship's captain stepped to the dock and bowed before the governor. He handed him a papyrus roll. Joseph watched curiously as the governor unrolled it, quickly read its contents, and stared hard at him. Then he glanced back at the letter, a puzzled look on his face. Feet widespread, hands on hips, he wore a stern look, but Joseph felt a smile lingered in the man's eyes.

A crewman grabbed Joseph and helped him off the bark. A guard beckoned to him and started into the compound. Joseph fell in behind him. A second guard followed closely. Joseph held his head and shoulders high as he walked past the prison governor. For the first time he became aware of the noise of metal clanging on metal.

The guard led him to a squalid hut. The dim interior, devoid of furniture, had a packed clay floor. Rolled pallets lined one wall. Compared to this, Joseph thought, Potiphar's slave quarters were palatial. The guard undid the ropes that bound him and pointed out a space along the wall. "This is where you sleep. Now follow me."

Joseph followed the guard through the compound. They stopped at a low-roofed building near the high tower. The keeper of the commissary issued him a woven-reed pallet, a single blanket, and a fired-clay food platter. He looked at them pensively. *I am twenty-seven years of age and this represents the extent of my earthly possessions – and they aren't even mine.*

The rest of the day passed slowly. Each succeeding day marched forward in wearisome sameness. Joseph discovered that, as a prisoner-slave, he had no rights whatsoever. Each morning he and the other prisoners awoke before light, ate stale bread or vermin-ridden fruit, then marched to the forges. The prison of Zawi-Re, Joseph discovered, was a huge metal works. Copper came in each week from a slave-run copper mine in the Sinai. Tin came by ship from Phoenicia. The foundry of Zawi-Re, run by prisoners under supervision of guards and metal workers, manufactured most of the bronze for the weaponry of the king's army. Forges burned day and night to turn ore into metal. In his pastoral existence, Joseph had never seen how metal was made. Now he took opportunity to learn something new.

Joseph's life had dramatically changed from rich to poor. Unbearable heat, vermin, ceaseless hunger, and varied forms of physical misery assailed him. But instead of each day being filled with bitterness, he made them days of growth and learning. Through his misery he developed a moral calm: a closeness to God. It was a great revelation to him of the real values of life. Here, deprived of the very basics, Joseph learned to fully appreciate what little he had: eating when hungry, drinking when thirsty, sleeping when sleepy, and talking when he desired to communicate with his fellow men.

Each day he worked from dawn to dark in the relentless sun. He used muscles he had not used in years. His skin blackened under the burning orb. His body leaned down to bare muscle, sinew, and bone. After two months in prison, his muscles toughened along with his faith. He started out assigned to pumping the bellows to keep the forges hot. After a short time he became foreman in charge of a forge. He treated fellow prisoners with respect, and set the goal that his forge turn out more metal than any other in the prison.

His father, Jacob, had pampered him, but serving Balshazar and Potiphar he had learned the value of hard work. Now he knew that hard work would help him succeed even here in the prison. Nefertekh had taught him the philosophy that the person who gets ahead is the one who does more than is necessary and keeps on doing it. Under Nefertekh's leadership, he also learned the value of delegating — that if a person tried to do it all, it would not get done. Now he put that learning to good use. The guards did not bother him or his men if they kept busy, and Joseph made sure they kept busy.

One day the prison governor stopped by the forge to watch their progress. He motioned to Joseph. "Come with me." Joseph obediently followed the governor to a building below the tower that was both office and residence. With a wave of his hand the governor bid Joseph to sit. Joseph looked expectantly at this man who had the power of life and death over him.

The governor smiled. "I am Amunebet, governor of the prison. I have watched you. In the time you have been here, I have heard nothing but good reports of you from the guards. In fact, your forge produced more bronze than any other." He waved a roll of papyrus at Joseph. "The king's prison holds many kinds of prisoners, but you are the first one who is here for attempting to bed the wife of one of Pharaoh's officers."

Joseph rose to protest, but Amunebet waved him down. "I know.

Potiphar indicates in his letter that he feels you are innocent." Then he added. "But how can one argue against a royal wife?" He laughed heartily. "Potiphar does say he misses your leadership on his estate." Joseph slumped in his chair.

"It is not in my power to release you, but Potiphar also informs me you are a keeper of records and have been his overseer. I can use those talents here." He unrolled the scroll to the bottom, then looked sadly at Joseph. "Potiphar also asks me to inform you that our friend, Nefertekh, died."

Joseph heard the words in silence. The news did not come as a surprise, but still saddened him. Nefertekh dead, who gave me such an education of life. He closed his eyes and leaned back. "Nefertekh was my mentor and dear friend. I leaned heavily on him for help and support during my first years in this new land. I will miss him greatly."

Amunebet respectfully waited. When Joseph opened his eyes, Amunebet commented. "Nefertekh was my friend, too. We served together in Pharaoh's army. I can tell he meant a great deal to you."

A tear glistened in Joseph's eye. "He befriended me. I was a slave, but he treated me as an equal."

"The embalmers are with him now. He will be given a burial in Potiphar's own tomb. His afterlife will be one of peace and tranquility."

In his ten years in Egypt, Joseph had come to understand somewhat the Egyptian feelings about death. His father had called Egypt the land of the dead. According to the Egyptians, the safety of the soul in the afterlife required the physical presence of the dead body. That must be why they spent so much time and energy with their rites of embalming. He noticed Amunebet looking intently at him. "I respect your traditions concerning the dead. I will miss Nefertekh."

"I will miss him, also, though it has been ten years since I last saw him. He paused. "But let's talk of you, now. I need help running this prison. I would like you to be my scribe, and perhaps later, the overseer. You would have the same responsibility here as you had at the home of Potiphar."

Joseph thought. Another change in my life! He bowed. "I will do all you ask me to do."

Within weeks, Joseph put the records in order, started teaching the prison scribes. Soon, Amunebet had him sending regular reports and accounts to the capital. With no special title or promotion, he became overseer and provisioner of the prison, answerable only to Amunebet. All records and accounts went through his hands. These seemed endless to Joseph. Government paperwork: forms for purchase of oil, corn, barley, and cattle; forms for giving supplies to the guards; a separate form for prisoner supplies; forms for operation of the foundry. There were even forms for transporting bronze goods to the capital.

"You are a man to be trusted," Amunebet said. "Though I cannot release you, I will do all I can do to make your life as comfortable as possible while in prison."

Tears came to Joseph's eyes. Amunebet reminded him of Nefertekh. "I will make sure your trust is not misplaced," Joseph said. "Perhaps we can even be friends."

"Friends?" Amunebet said sadly. "I have not had a friend since leaving the army. Ten years in this hell-hole — no friends, no relationships, no time off. I hate being a jailer."

"It seems to me that you have little more freedom than the prisoners," Joseph remarked. "My most precious possession is freedom."

"How can you be so eloquent about freedom, when you really don't have any?"

Joseph smiled. "Usually those deprived of something appreciate it most."

"True. But are you sure what freedom really is."

Joseph was never at a loss for words when it came to freedom. "One aspect of freedom is thinking."

Amunebet paced in the small room where they lunched. "Just thinking? I think of freedom as the ability to go where you want to go; To do what you want to do; To be what you want to be."

"It is all of that, my lord. But without the power to think, none of those have any value. To go anywhere without truly thinking and seeing is worth nothing. Doing only what one wants to do, without consideration for others can be not only a waste of one's time, but might even be detrimental to God's purposes. There must be purpose, and purpose only comes through thinking. Being what you want to be might destroy the very freedom you espouse. I heard someone say he would like to be a dog — to just lie around and not have any worries. You may call that freedom, but I do not."

"God gives freedom?"

"God gives us the power and ability to think." Joseph enjoyed these verbal interchanges with Amunebet. It helped him solidify his own beliefs.

Amunebet paused before speaking. "You speak of God. I believe we are children of our god, Osiris."

Joseph nodded. "Many people have that inborn feeling — that we do have a Heavenly Father. That is what makes each person valuable. That feeling of value gives freedom to plan, to devise and dream. Nothing then is impossible to us. Horizons of limitation are swept back, and ever back."

"You feel thinking is so important. Is a person who produces a new idea more important than the person who produces through his own physical labor. "

Joseph shrugged. "Both are important, but physical labor can extend no further than the now. The man who does no more than physical labor, consumes his own contribution and leaves no further value, either for himself or others. But the man who produces an idea, the man who discovers new knowledge, benefits all humanity."

Amunebet shook his head. "That is not necessarily true. The pyramids of Egypt are a good example of physical labor lasting forever as a monument to man."

Joseph conceded, though he would have liked to bring forth the idea that even the pyramids existed as an idea before they took physical shape. What he said was, "That is true. I am glad someone had the freedom to plan and then to carry out those plans."

Amunebet was not through. "Freedom needs to be guarded continuously. It needs to be cherished and never taken for granted."

Smiling sadly, Joseph spoke cryptically. "From my position I would say that is a true statement."

"Please excuse me," Amunebet cried. "I did not mean to intrude on your sensitivities. If I had my way, you would be a free man."

"I know it," Joseph said gently. "I am not bitter. God will use me, even as a prisoner of Pharaoh, to accomplish His purposes. How, I do not know. But remember, I still have the freedom to choose my thoughts and my attitudes. No king, no Pharaoh, no prison governor, can take that from me."

Chapter 9: Butler and Baker

Amunebet came to Joseph's room cursing under his breath. Joseph waited for him to calm down.

"What is it?"

"We received two 'special' guests today. They are to be shown extra privileges and given a special room of their own." He mumbled something unintelligible.

"What?"

"Oh, I just said that if Pharaoh wanted them to have special privileges, why didn't he keep them at the palace? I am not running a pleasure resort on this island."

"Who are they?"

"The Pharaoh's personal cup bearer and baker."

"Why are they here?"

"Oh, there was some rumor at the palace about a plan to poison the Pharaoh. These two were implicated in some way. Personally, I don't think either of them has brains enough to conspire against the throne." He looked at Joseph and laughed out loud. "Since they need special treatment, I assign you as their steward. You will take food to them and do whatever else is needed to entertain them."

Joseph shrugged his acceptance, though he questioned Amunebet's wisdom in assigning him such a task.

"Aren't you even going to ask me why?"

Joseph said, "Why should I ask? You are the governor. I am the prisoner."

"I have done this hoping that if these men are released, they will take a good word about you to Pharaoh. Through them you may gain your freedom."

Joseph started to say something, then simply nodded. "Thank you."

He went to see the two servants of Pharaoh. As he approached their hut the guards smiled at him and raised their spears in salute. Joseph knew he had earned their respect. They liked him. They drew back the heavy wooden bolt from the door and Joseph entered. Coming from the glare of the sun, it took a moment for his eyes to get used to the gloomy dimness.

Two men, their heads in their hands, sat in a corner. Joseph bowed. "The governor assigned me to be your servant. Is there anything I can do for you?"

The two men looked at him. Then they stood. They appeared quite morose. In the dimly-lighted room, Joseph could see that one was short and plump with huge jowls and purple-red cheeks, an untidy beard, bright lips, and dark sardonic eyes — eyes now shot with crimson as if he had spent a miserable night — as well he probably had. He was so fat he waddled when he walked. The other man was tall and stooped. A fringe of black hair framed his sallow face. He had a long nose and a sagging, unpleasant mouth. He gave the impression of being always ready to offer a sour comment or a sad expression.

"My name is Joseph. I will serve your meals and attend to your needs. If you desire anything, just ask, and if I can, I will provide it."

The tall man stood back aloof, but the fat one came up to Joseph. "Oh, this is so terrible," he said. "Me, the chief butler of the great Pharaoh — in prison." He wrung his hands as he spoke. Joseph could see he verged on tears.

"Why are you sent to prison?" Joseph asked.

The butler looked at the baker, then answered. "We attended a dinner meeting for the king and his courtiers. I served the wine for the Pharaoh, and Sineb ..." he pointed at the baker "... served the bread." He shook his head in wonderment. "I do not know what happened, but the vizier found flies in the wine and stones of nitre in Sineb's bread." His eyes brimmed. "We are accused of trying to poison Pharaoh." He ducked his head to hide his emotions.

Joseph turned to the baker. "Did you attempt to poison the Pharaoh?"

The baker's mouth tightened and his eyes flared. "That is absurd! We are loyal to the king."

Joseph shrugged and turned to leave. "Remember, if you need something, please let me know." He turned and left the hut. A guard shut the door behind him. Joseph winked at him. This assignment was going to be interesting.

Over the next few months, Joseph and Mut, the butler, became close friends. The baker remained aloof and refused to join in conversation. Mut, a jovial person, visited for hours with Joseph. He talked of life in the palace and about the Pharaoh. It was good information for Joseph. In turn, Joseph told Mut about his youth in Canaan, of grass-covered hills and groves of trees. He told him of his service to Potiphar and of Zelicah. Mut clucked sympathetically.

The prison, with his help, ran smoothly. That gave Joseph additional time to pursue his own interests. Since assuming the position of chief scribe and overseer, Joseph had started a personal journal — a record of his experiences. Each day he wrote what had happened. One night, as he slept, he had a dream. He dreamed he was back at the forge, making metal from copper and tin ores. After he poured the molten metal from the crucible, he hammered it into thin sheets — even thinner that those they made as coverings for Pharaoh's war chariots. He awoke from his dream, wondering about its meaning.

He had always been a dreamer. Through dreams, the Lord had continued to instruct him. What did this dream mean? He lay there, thinking, and soon slept again. This time he saw himself in his office, but instead of a reed brush in his hand, he inscribed with a stylus on the metal plates. He awoke, his eyes wide with understanding. The lord wanted him to do his writing on plates — something which would last through time. He raised himself and knelt on the pallet. "What is it, Lord? What would you have me do?"

The peaceful feeling he knew so well once again came over him. A voice spoke to him — spoke words of instruction. "Write a record of my people. But write on plates of bronze so they may be preserved for later generations. You shall be My prophet and shall teach My people."

The next day Joseph went back to the forges. He watched as metalworkers fashioned large sheets of bronze, hammered thin to be used as armor on the king's chariots. Joseph drew the chief metalworker aside and instructed him to make him bronze plates as thin as the papyrus they wrote upon. The metalworker looked at him quizzically, but he obeyed. Soon, Joseph had his plates.

He sat in his office, stylus in hand. Writing upon the new plates thrilled him. For weeks he wrote of his own life, of his dreams and his youth; of the perfidy of his brothers, and of the promises the Lord had made him. He wrote of his love for Jacob, his father. Then he started writing down the oral traditions his father taught him — of the creation of man, of Adam and Eve, of Noah and Shem, of his great-grandfather Abraham, of Sariah, of Isaac — his grandfather — and of Jacob, his father, known as Israel. Carefully, he started to chronicle the history of God's chosen people from Adam through the flood down to his own time. He knew now, with certainty, one of the One God's purposes for him.

Joseph entered the prison cell to find both Mut and Sineb frowning. He asked, "Why so sad?"

Mut responded morosely. "We each dreamed a dream and we don't know what they mean."

"I may be able to help you," Joseph said. "God has given me power to interpret dreams. Tell me your dream and perhaps God shall give you an interpretation." He prayed silently for God's help.

The butler eagerly said, "In my dream I beheld a large vine. On the vine I saw three branches. The vine blossomed and soon reached a great height. Its clusters ripened and became grapes. I took the grapes, pressed them in a cup, and placed it in Pharaoh's hand, and he drank." He looked at Joseph expectantly.

Joseph stood silent for a moment experiencing that sweet mystery of interpretation given by the Lord. He responded. "The three branches upon the vine represent three days. In three days the king will order you released and will restore you to your office." Joseph paused and looked at the fat butler. "Mut, when you are back at Pharaoh's court, remember me to Pharaoh. Have me freed from this prison. I have told you how traders stole me away from the land of Canaan and sold me as a slave. Also, I am innocent of any offense against Potiphar or his wife."

Mut nodded happily. "If the king frees me as you say, I will get you out of this prison."

The baker, Sineb, had stood at the back of the hut. Now he stepped forward. "Will you interpret my dream?"

"I can interpret no dream by myself," Joseph said. "But if the Lord desires, and will work through me, then we can find an interpretation."

The baker related. "In my dream I saw three white baskets upon my head. In the uppermost basket were all manner of baked meats for Pharaoh. But the birds came and ate them from off my head."

Joseph did not answer for several minutes. Then he shivered and looked at Sineb, reluctant to tell the baker the interpretation. Then he said bluntly, "I am sorry, Sineb, but the three baskets which you saw are three days. In three days Pharaoh will take off your head, and hang your body upon a tree, and the birds will eat your flesh."

Sineb shrank back, his hand to his mouth. His eyes, whites showing strangely in the dimness, filled with fear. "What are you saying?" he cried, hiding his face in his hands.

"I'm sorry," Joseph said.

Mut went to his friend, placed a hand on his shoulder, and attempted to comfort him.

Joseph, also upset, bowed and turned to leave.

Mut shouted, "Wait." He waddled to the door and whispered,

"Thank you."

Joseph walked back in the bright sunshine to the governor's house. "Why, Lord? Why is one saved and the other not?" An impression came to him. The one will have influence with Pharaoh in your behalf. The other will not.

Three days passed. A ship pulled into the dock. A messenger from Pharaoh jumped from the ship and took his message directly to Amunebet. Amunebet looked at Joseph, a new respect in his eyes. "It is as you predicted. Mut is to be freed and Sineb is to be executed."

Joseph walked with Amunebet to Mut's place of confinement. Sineb shrieked as Mut left him alone. "Do not leave me, Mut. Tell Pharaoh I am innocent."

Leaving the baker in the prison hut, Joseph walked with Mut to the river. "Soon you will be surrounded by friends. I am proud to be the first to congratulate you upon being found innocent." Before the fat butler boarded the boat, Joseph asked again, "Please think of me when you are before Pharaoh. Please call to his attention that I am innocent of that of which I am accused."

Mut grabbed his two hands. "Yes, I will tell him. I promise that I will mention you at the first opportunity when I stand before Pharaoh. I will remind him each time I can. My friend, you will receive your pardon." As the ship pulled away from the dock, Joseph waved. Then he walked back to his room. He kept his eyes downcast since he had no desire to see the woeful scarecrow figure of the baker, Sineb, whose body dangled from a tree outside the walls.

Justice had been swift, but remembrance was slow. Joseph continued working, but his thoughts often dwelt on Mut, the butler. Apparently he has forgotten all about me. It has been two years since he was freed — two years of frustration. *Oh, God, but I long to be free.* He prayed. *Father, though I have despaired, I have never given up hope. Perhaps you are just giving me time to fulfill Your purposes — to record the history of Your people.*

Chapter 10: Before Pharoah

Shouts of excitement drew Joseph's attention. Hurrying outside he saw guards and prisoners clustered near the river. Amunebet called, "It is the Pharaoh's private bark." He joined Joseph as they made their way through the island prison to the docking area. The bark, with curving lotus prow, purple sail, and bearing the royal seal had just docked. Amunebet said, "It is an express boat from Pharaoh's private fleet."

A slender youth leaped ashore. He pushed his way through the crowd, a look of urgency on his lean face. He called to an onlooker. "I seek Amunebet, the prison governor." The servant pointed. The youth approached Amunebet and Joseph, bowed low, then repeated, "I seek Amunebet, the prison governor."

"You have found me."

The youth pulled a papyrus scroll from his belt and handed it to Amunebet. The governor glanced through it, then looked at Joseph. "It concerns you, Joseph," he said. "Pharaoh desires that you stand before him at once."

"But why?"

"The letter does not say. You are just commanded to go to him immediately."

Joseph looked wildly around him, then glanced down at his cotton skirt. Self-consciously he stroked his beard. "I will have to shave and wash up ... and my hair ... I'll need to put on clean clothes." The runner interrupted. "You can do that aboard ship. We must make haste. Pharaoh waits."

"At least let me get my things." Joseph put his arm through Amunebet's arm and turned him towards his hut. "What do you think it means?" he whispered. "Will I come back here? What shall I do?"

Amunebet shrugged. "I know not, but the will of the Pharaoh is the will of the Pharaoh."

In his quarters Joseph gathered his few belongings — the rolls of his precious papyrus journal in which he kept his daily notes, ink bottles, and reed pens. Carefully he lifted the plates of bronze upon which he had so prayerfully written over the past three years. He lovingly put them in a leather bag. They were his only possession of worth, but they were worth much.

He stepped back into the bright sunlight. Amunebet stood where he had left him. The runner paced anxiously. Joseph gripped Amunebet's right hand and put a hand on his shoulder. Tears filled his eyes as he spoke. "My friend, you have been a brother to me these three years. In fact, you have taken the place of the father who gave me up for dead so many years ago." He squeezed his shoulder, then at the insistent urging of the anxious messenger, walked quickly to the bark.

They had no more than leaped aboard than the ship pulled into the river. Manned by five oarsmen on either side, the bark fairly flew across the water. The runner introduced himself as Yen, one of Pharaoh's chief messengers. He pulled Joseph under the pavilion on the after deck. Joseph was surprised to find a tub there, filled with warm water. No one needed to urge him. He stripped his clothes off and holding the edge of the tub, lowered himself into the tepid water. It felt so good. Baths at the prison consisted of morning swims in the muddy Nile. Sometimes he felt he came out of the water dirtier than he had gone in. Now he luxuriated in the bath.

While Joseph bathed, a servant got rid of Joseph's clothes and placed fresh ones near the tub. Yen stood nearby, talking the entire time.

"Where are we going?" Joseph interrupted.

"To the royal palace at On."

"I thought the royal palace is in Avaris."

"The Pharaoh and his beautiful consort have gone to On in their ship, Star of Two Lands, to celebrate one of the many religious festivals. The Pharaoh maintains a palace there as well as at Avaris and Thebes." Yen rattled on about the festivities in On. "Pharaoh is installing a new chief priest for worship of the sun god, Ra."

The politics of Egypt did not interest Joseph. He interrupted the messenger again. "Do you know why Pharaoh sent for me?"

"Oh, have you not heard?" Yen replied. "Pharaoh dreamed some dreams. He sent for you to interpret them."

"Dreams?"

"Yes. Rumors at the court are that the chief butler of Pharaoh recommended you as an interpreter of dreams."

Joseph sighed. *It has been two years since I interpreted the dreams of Mut. But he finally remembered me. The Lord continues to work in his mysterious ways. There is still a reward for service.*

Yen talked on. Joseph became aware of what he was saying. "… some weird dream of seven skinny cows coming out of the river and eating seven fat cows." He shrugged. "If you cannot interpret them you won't be alone. Pharaoh has already had all the court astrologers and wise men suggest interpretations. But none of the interpretations satisfied him."

Shutting from his mind the rambling of the young messenger, he concentrated on the dream. *Seven cows eating seven cows? What could it mean?* He silently prayed. *Father, you have blessed me with the gift of knowing men's dreams. Grant me the understanding of Pharaoh's dream.*

After his bath, a valet shaved him with a sharp bronze razor, then rubbed him with oil and perfume. Joseph dressed in a clean white cotton skirt, sandals laced to the knee, and a leather harness which fit over his shoulders. It felt good to be clean-shaven again. The valet held up a polished bronze mirror. Joseph slowly inspected himself. At thirty, he was a handsome man. His face and hands had whitened somewhat from his indoor work at the prison: gone was the dark tan that had made him look so much like an Egyptian. He no longer had a well-fed look. He was lean. Large brooding eyes dominated his face — eyes that would have reminded Jacob of Rachel. He had a warm, full mouth and a certain air of self-assurance. From his service to Potiphar and the governor of the prison, he had learned graciousness in his manners.

They docked at mid-afternoon. The city of On lay where the Nile divided into two separate rivers. Joseph could see houses and streets that formed a triangle whose tip coincided with the apex where the two rivers divided. At that spot, a magnificent obelisk reared above the surrounding buildings. Gold-covered surfaces met in a point at the top, reflecting the bright rays of the afternoon sun. Looking at the obelisk blinded him. The whole city gleamed, reflecting the beneficent rays of the sun which the people worshipped. He thought of that day, thirteen years before when Balshazar's caravan had passed On. So much had happened since then.

Joseph and his attendants hurried from the dock to the palace. The bustle of this huge city continued to intrigue him. Three years of forced exile had created within him a hunger — a hunger for people and their common-day activities. People in their finery filled the square before the palace. Groups of soldiers and charioteers stood before the walled gate to keep away the loiterers.

Peddlers selling sweetmeats and cakes moved through the crowd. Booths displayed statues and scarabs along one wall. The scene reminded Joseph of many other feast days and markets he had seen during his service to Potiphar. Yet, he felt something different about this one — almost an undercurrent of anxiety among the people.

"Make way. Make way for the king's messenger," Yen shouted as the guards shouldered through the crowds. A servant, apparently waiting for them, stepped forward from the gates. He conferred briefly with Yen, then led them through the gate toward the inner court. A court official motioned frantically for them to hurry. Joseph ignored the glances of curiosity which followed him. He busied himself looking at the glimmering glory of the halls and rooms.

They made their way through a gaily-painted vestibule, the walls decorated with landscapes and the columns wound with festive ribbons. Turning into a hall decorated with highly-polished woods, they almost bumped into a troop of armed man standing before a wide door — the entrance to the great hall, the throne room of the Pharaoh. A hush settled over the group. Joseph found himself pushed to the front and towards the door.

The doors of the great hall swung open. Joseph looked in awe at the huge room. Great alabaster pillars held up the ceiling, which had been painted to look like the blue sky — including birds in flight. The throne sat on a dais at one end. Surrounding the throne a large group of people talked and gestured. As Joseph entered, an expectant hush settled over the group. Silently Joseph prayed, "El Shaddai, let me feel your power."

On the throne, in the midst of the courtiers, sat the Pharaoh, King of the Two Lands. The double crown sat on his head. Golden ties held the ceremonial beard of royalty to his youthful chin. A cobra diadem dominated his forehead. His hands held the symbols of his kingship — the Crook and Flail. Joseph estimated the young Pharaoh to be about the age he had been when sold to the slave traders — about seventeen or eighteen. The Pharaoh gazed over the heads of his courtiers, half listening. As Joseph entered the hall, he sat straighter in his royal chair, a look of interest in his face.

The Pharaoh, though young, carried an aura of age. Possibly, thought Joseph, because of his great responsibilities. Joseph noticed his well-developed chin, his royal, high-arched nose, the full lips and deep, thoughtful eyes, half-hidden by long lashes. Joseph walked slowly forward until he stood directly before the throne, bowed low, and said as he had been instructed: "O Lord of Beauty, King of the Two Lands, your servant awaits your command." He raised his eyes.

Pharaoh lifted himself from his seat, clutching the arms of the throne. His knuckles stood out white. His air was one of tense expectancy. Veiled eyes widened as he looked down at Joseph.

Joseph kept his eyes about level with Pharaoh's feet. He noticed the ornate lion's feet of the throne chair; Pharaoh's small feet, even the ornate gold sandal strap between Pharaoh's toes. He heard the command, "Stand." Rising to his feet he stood eye level with the great king.

The Pharaoh looked at Joseph, a hopeful expression on his face. He spoke. "I am told you are an interpreter of dreams."

"Great king, I am only the mouthpiece of my God. He alone has power to read men's minds and interpret their dreams."

"Which God gives you such aid? You are from the land eastward from which my forefathers came. Is your God Baal?"

"No, Great King. He is the One God. He is the great *I AM*."

The Pharaoh waved his hand as if Joseph's answer was irrelevant. "But you do interpret dreams?"

"Yes, Great King."

Relieved, the Pharaoh leaned back in his chair. With a wave of his hand he signaled the aged vizier who stood to one side of the dais leaning on his staff. The vizier rapped the staff on the floor, sending the people from the room. Joseph and the old man stood alone before Pharaoh.

The Pharaoh spoke urgently. "Let me tell you my dreams. In my first dream I stood on the river bank. It was a lonely, marshy uncultivated place. While I stood there, the river bubbled and rippled, then seven cows came out of the water and walked to the shore." The young Pharaoh paused, showing his perplexity. "They had probably been lying in the water like buffalo cows. They came out of the water moving one after another in a straight line — almost as if marching — one behind the other, seven cows. Magnificent cows, — white ones, black ones, gray ones, and two dappled ones. They were fat with bursting udders, long-lashed eyes, and lyre-shaped horns. I would have liked to have them in my own pasture. They grazed contentedly on the shore. I have never seen such sleek, well-fed cattle. Even though it was a dream, my heart rejoiced at the sight."

Pharaoh's voice changed. Wonderment and concern sharpened his voice. "Seven more cows came out of the water, joining the first seven. I shuddered when I saw these, the ugliest, leanest, most starveling cows I had ever seen. Bones stood out on their wrinkled hides, udders were like empty bags with string-like teats. Those cows were an alarming and upsetting sight. They seemed scarcely able to stand. They aggressively advanced on the fat cows, leapt on their backs, and devoured them." The young Pharaoh shook his head. "But even after eating the fat cows, the lean cows remained lean. There was no sign they were any fuller." He sighed. "The dream ended, but it was so vivid I awakened, shuddering and perspiring. For some time I lay awake, thinking about what I had dreamed." Pharaoh looked distraught. Beads of perspiration stood out on his forehead.

Joseph wisely waited.

Pharaoh continued. "When I fell asleep again, I dreamed again I stood on the bank of the river. But on the bank lay a strip of plowed, black earth. As I watched, a green corn stalk pierced the crust and rose above the soil. As it grew, seven ears of corn broke forth, one after another. They were full, fat ears, bursting with golden fullness. But as the stalk kept growing, seven more ears — poor, pathetic, dead and dry, blackened with mildew and blight — pushed out raggedly below the full ears. Then the great, full ears just seemed to vanish into the lean ones. Truly it was like that. The wretched ears swallowed up the fat ones. And like the cows, they were no fuller, no fatter than before." He sat straight in his chair, firmly grasping its arms. Through tight lips, he asked Joseph, "What does it mean?"

Joseph stood with bowed head, silently asking for divine help. Then he spoke. "There is only one dream, though you dreamed it twice. The second dream came only to give precise meaning to the first. The meaning of the dream is also single. The One God revealed this dream to Pharaoh so he can prepare for the future survival of his people in the Two Lands — a future foretold Pharaoh in his dreams."

Impatiently, Pharaoh asked, "But what means my dreams. Tell me."

Joseph spoke slowly. "The cows are years, passing one after another before the mighty king. The first seven cows represent seven fat years which will come to Egypt. These fat years will be followed by seven lean years — years when there will be such a want the people will forget the seven good years. Famine will consume the land. Then, just as the lean cows consumed the fat, and the blasted ears the golden ones, the famine's harshness will consume the people's memory of the full ones." He paused. "Great King, that is the interpretation of your dream."

Pharaoh sat unmoving, unconsciously chewing on his upper lip. Joseph could see that the burden of decision grew heavy on him. He muttered, "I see. I see." He turned to the vizier. "This is the correct interpretation." Turning back to Joseph, he said, "I called the royal astrologers, every soothsayer in Egypt, and all the wise men from the city to interpret my dreams. Each one looked at me blankly after I told them my dream." He chuckled. "Several of them gave wondering head shakes, and said such things as, 'They are wonderful dreams, unique dreams.' None were able to give a true meaning to my dreams. And now . . ." He turned to the old vizier. "We need a plan. What should we do first?"

The old man stood silent, apparently not sure how to respond to the king.

Joseph interrupted. "Great King. May I respectfully suggest that you do have time — at least seven years. That will give time to avert any calamity. You will be able to note the coming evil days and work against it. Because of your advance knowledge, you will not only be able to keep the calamity in bounds, but you may derive blessings from it as well."

Pharaoh asked suspiciously, "Blessings? What do you mean?"

"If Pharaoh will heap up provisions and gather them into his bins and granaries, he will become the benefactor of the land. Not only will people praise him, but in the process, he will become ever more wealthy."

Pharaoh nodded. "I am grateful that the dreams show the good times first — not the bad times."

"Yes, if God had put the bad time first, there would be no time for planning. There is time, but none to waste. Steps must be taken to prepare for the time of want."

"What steps?"

"Pharaoh should first find a man, discreet and wise, and set him over the land of Egypt. Then Pharaoh should appoint officers over the land, and store a portion of every harvest during the seven plenteous years."

"But how is this to be done?"

"Bins and storehouses must be built on the largest possible scale. Each city in the Two Lands must have its own storage facilities. The master in charge of the gathering must be able to control storage and distribution with strictness. He must be committed to his task. He must have Pharaoh's power behind him so the people will follow his direction."

Pharaoh said, "Do you think that without any loss of time I should summon my advisors to a council so they may decide how to deal with the abundance to make it serve the lean years."

Joseph spoke wryly. "If I may be so bold as to suggest it, Pharaoh seems to have had little success with councils he called to help him interpret his dreams. The problems of the next fourteen years are of such magnitude that perhaps Pharaoh alone is worthy to decide and execute what must be done."

Joseph's eyes chanced to meet the eyes of the old vizier standing beside the throne. Shrewd, sharp eyes, gleaming black out of the shadow.

The old man's lips shaped a mocking smile. Joseph quickly dropped his eyes to the floor but he could not hold back a smile of his own. He knew the vizier would have to have his say. His position had been threatened.

The vizier growled. "Amenhotep, the Pharaoh, decides all policies for the Two Lands, but he assigns others to execute his policies."

Joseph feared he had already said too much. He looked carefully at the old counselor, then back at the Pharaoh. "Please excuse my ignorance of your customs," he said, bowing slightly. "My father in his own land would decide and execute his own orders. However, I still suggest that Pharaoh look for a wise and understanding man in whom dwells the spirit of Pharaoh's dreams, and set him over the Two Lands. Give him authority to administer the abundance of the years of plenty. Then, during the lean years, the king's subjects will praise the mighty king for his foresight." Feeling his audience was over, he bowed low and turned to go.

Pharaoh said, "Stay."

Joseph turned back, a quizzical look on his face.

Pharaoh sat silent, chin cupped in his small hands. He looked up. "I cannot let you go unrewarded." He paused, then looked up. "By what name are you called?"

"Joseph."

"Joseph, why were you in the king's prison?"

Joseph had no desire to get Potiphar in trouble, but the truth must he told. He recounted to Pharaoh the sordid details of Zelicah's flirtation with him. He ended with, "And so, my lord, Potiphar had no choice but to cast me into the prison. It is not proper to doubt the word of one's wife."

"You talk as a husband. Are you married?"

"No, great king."

"If you were part of my court, I would marry you off. I would even choose your bride." He smiled, a look of chagrin on his face. "But you are not part of my court." He stopped. A glimmer of a smile played around his lips.

"How long have you been in the prison?"

"Three years."

"And in Potiphar's service?"

"Ten years."

Again Amenhotep pursed his lips. "Since you have been in prison, you are probably not aware of what has happened to Potiphar."

"No, great king."

"You noticed the festivities outside the palace?" Joseph nodded.

"I have rewarded Potiphar for his years of faithful service by appointing him High Priest of On."

Joseph smiled his pleasure. "He is worthy of your appointment. His loyalty to you is beyond question."

Pharaoh seemed pleased with Joseph's answer. "You seem to be a person of skill and discernment. Moments ago you mentioned your father as being a man who could not only make decisions but execute them. Tell me about your father and why you are now a slave."

Joseph looked at the floor, hardly knowing where to start. He shut his eyes, holding back tears that threatened to erupt as he thought of his aged father — who by now had probably been laid to rest in the cave at Machpelah. He hand went unconsciously to the small leather bag hanging from his neck. "Great Pharaoh, my father is a chieftain and worshipper of the One God in the land of Canaan. He has twelve sons and many flocks and herds. I was sold by my jealous brothers to a caravan journeying to the Two Lands. The caravan master sold me to Potiphar."

"Why would your One God permit such a thing to happen?"

"He told me that in your land I would be able to perform a mission of saving my own people."

Pharaoh leaned forward in his chair, then stepped down from the dais. He walked around Joseph, hands clasped behind his back. He stopped facing Joseph. "Your God would permit you to be a slave and a prisoner for thirteen years? Thirteen years to lose your identity?"

"I believe, great king, that only by aligning our wills with God's is full happiness to be found. The thirteen years might not be a question of losing one's identity, but of finding his true identity, if it were to suit God's purposes."

"And what do you think this god's purposes to be?"

"I don't know," Joseph replied, "but I trust His judgment."

Amenhotep smiled. "In Egypt we have many gods. Your god — who or what is He?"

Carefully wording his reply, Joseph answered. "The God I worship is the One God — the unseen God. He is the God of my father. My great-grandfather Abraham made a covenant with the One God that we would always be His people and would worship no other gods."

Pharaoh returned to his throne. "And this forefather of yours discovered this god?" He leaned forward in his chair, his fingers squeezing and kneading his chin. "Is the One God the sun's disk?"

"No, great king," Joseph answered. "The God whom he worshipped and taught my father of is much more than the sun's disk. He is our own Heavenly Father."

Pharaoh seemed intensely interested. He said, as if to himself. "Then it is possible that your One God sent you to me to interpret my dreams." He was interrupted by his aged vizier who stepped forward until he stood directly before the throne. "It seems to be great Amenhotep, that your soothsayer has been called forth from the dungeon — not from any god of his own fabrication."

Pharaoh stretched forth his hand, silencing the old counselor. There was a puzzled look in his eyes. "Perhaps. Or maybe Joseph's One God has brought him to me at this time for a purpose." He turned back to Joseph. "You say this god of yours is a Heavenly Father. I, too, feel that my god, my own father, is a heavenly father." He looked at the old counselor. "I feel my heavenly father sent Joseph to me from prison to save our people." He clapped his hands. A servant appeared and dropped to his knees before the throne. "Summon my scribe."

Almost instantaneously a door opened and a thickset man entered carrying a scribe's pallets and ink pots. He seated himself cross-legged on the edge of the raised platform, swiftly removed lids from two little pots on a board, snatched a pointed reed from behind his ear and produced a roll of papyrus. He sat, reed poised.

"Joseph, tell me what you think we should do."

As Joseph spoke, Amenhotep motioned to the scribe, who wrote everything he said.

"Great Pharaoh," Joseph began. "There cannot be enough barns and granaries already built to handle surpluses over the next years. New ones must be built everywhere so that their number cannot be counted. Officers of Pharaoh must be appointed to supervise the harvest. A fair tax must be assessed upon everyone so that grain in Pharaoh's granaries may be numbered until it is like the sands of the desert. Provision must be made for bins and granaries near the cities so food is laid up for distribution during the lean years. Under this plan no one will perish from hunger. Distribution would be to the poor of the cities, but grain would be sold to those who can afford it. Thus will Pharaoh increase in stature before the people."

Pharaoh looked skeptical. "But who would organize such a program?"

"You would have to find and appoint a wise and understanding man," Joseph answered. "One filled with the spirit of planning and foresight. The all-wise Pharaoh will have to seek out this man from among his servants. The man must also be one who can see beyond the borders of this land. It is he who would supervise the building of the barns, the directing of the officials, the enforcing of laws governing the collection of taxes. He shall investigate and determine to whom grain shall be given and to whom it shall be sold. He shall arrange that the poor shall eat and yet that Pharaoh's wealth shall increase.

The old counselor sputtered and started to speak, but Pharaoh silenced him with a wave of his hand. "Tell me more, my dream interpreter. Since we are in council, tell me more about this man who should be appointed." Joseph shrugged. "I am not an Egyptian, but I have studied this land during the thirteen years I have lived here. I feel I know the people and their needs. If I were to suggest the duties of such a man as is needed as overseer, I would say he would fix the prices of the harvest for the seven full years. Those who resist would pay with taxes, so that grain could be purchased and stored."

Pharaoh chuckled.

The old vizier did not seem to think of it as being funny. He asked, "But what of the temples? They are rich to excess. Shall this overseer harass them, too, and cause them to pay taxes or grain?"

Aware that the old man attempted to trap him, Joseph responded carefully. "No, if the man chosen as overseer is wise, he will spare the temples and leave the gods of Egypt alone during the years of plenty. The gods must not be vexed against the work of provision and storage of supplies. When the hard times come, then the temple will have to pay the prices of the master. Pharaoh shall profit greatly from the entire fourteen years if the overseer acts wisely."

"Very sensible," muttered the vizier.

"There is one more concern," Joseph added. "When my great-grandfather Abraham came down to Egypt with his wife Sarai there was famine in his country. In Egypt there was plenty. Shall it be different this time?"

"What do you suggest?" Pharaoh asked.

"The famine will not affect Egypt alone. I think it would be important that the person chosen as overseer be aware that many people from lands outside the borders of Egypt will seek grain. People from everywhere will come here and say, 'Sell to us.' The peoples of these lands will pay dearly for the grain you can provide them."

Amenhotep smiled broadly. This seemed more and more to his liking, more as if dreams would turn the fortunes of the world to him. He turned to the vizier. "Pepy-nakhte, our court is fully staffed. We have two viziers, overseer of the granaries and the king's herds, and the chief scribe of the treasury. What would be the title of this new overseer?"

Pepy-nakhte, the vizier, shrugged. "Traditions of earlier times tell of an officer, a grand vizier, between the Pharaoh and the chief officials of state."

The king stood, very solemn. "Come here, Joseph."

Joseph stepped to the edge of the platform.

The small Pharaoh, standing on the dais, was about level with him. He put a hand on Joseph's shoulder, and looked him in the eye. "Joseph, you are the one. I have listened to you. I have watched you carefully while you have been before me. You shall be my chief advisor. You shall be my grand vizier, the overseer of all the Two Lands. Upon you shall the highest power be given. Only I will be greater in the land."

Joseph bowed his head. His knees felt weak, and for a moment he was light-headed. Thoughts flowed through his mind. So this is the way the One God would use me. Now I begin to fully understand. I had to learn to submit to the hand of the Lord and to acknowledge his hand in all things. God needed to melt my pride away by scorching me with humiliation as a slave and prisoner.

The Pharaoh continued. "Your God told you the answer to my dreams. He showed you how to prepare for the years of famine. You shall be over this people. My people shall be obedient to your word. Because of your great wisdom, I change your name to Psothom-Phanech." Observing Joseph's silence, he asked, "Are you surprised? Will you accept?"

Joseph knelt on the floor before this kindly monarch. "Great King, I bow to your wishes. I promise you that I will serve you with every bit of energy I possess. I prayed that I might invest my life to do the most good for mankind. God, through you, has provided a way."

The Pharaoh acted excited. He motioned to the scribe. "Let it be known that this day I hereby give manumission to Joseph." Turning, he said, "Joseph, you are no longer a slave, but a free man." He could hardly contain his excitement. "Not only a free man, but second to Pharaoh alone in power in the Two Lands. In your hands shall be all the lands of Egypt." He pulled a ring from his finger. "Here, wear this. It will be a symbol of your power. He motioned Joseph to sit on the step before him. "Only by the height of the royal throne shall I be greater than you."

Chapter 11: Grand Visier of Egypt

Amenhotep insisted that Joseph stay in the palace. Attendants ushered him to a room in the Pharaoh's wing — a small room, but gracefully proportioned. Vari-colored rugs softened the polished clay floor. Walls were a delicate peach color and decorated with animal pictures. Adjoining the room a bedchamber contained an alcove for a lion-headed bed. A deep, upholstered chair of scarlet leather stood in one corner. When Joseph entered, a servant greeted him with an armful of clothes — not the common cotton ones, but real, finely textured linen.

One door in his room opened onto the garden. After the sun sank below the western walls of the palace, Joseph ventured out. The garden was spacious, green and cool. A pavilion stood in the center beside a pool with gently waving reeds at one end. Tall acacia trees shaded gravel paths. Tamarisk trees circled the pool. The overall effect was one of calmness and peace. Fragrances of varieties of flowers filled Joseph's nostrils. He sat by the pool on a stone bench, watching the ever expanding ripples as fish surfaced and disappeared.

He wondered about his new position, overwhelmed as he thought about it. The ripples in the water reminded him that he would have to delegate many tasks. His influence would have a ripple effect — would expand through appointment of others whom he could trust — men who would be loyal to him. He was grateful for his experience as overseer in Potiphar's household and the experience he had gained running the prison under Amunebet's able direction. He snapped his fingers. That was it. He would ask for Amunebet to be his chief assistant. What an asset he would be. Already he felt easier in his mind.

As day darkened, Joseph glanced around the garden again, not wanting it to fade from memory. He made his way slowly to his room. Candles threw a soft light. A basin of warm water sat on a stand near the door. How circumstances changed. Yesterday I slept on a mat in a prison. Tonight I will sleep on a raised bed in the palace of the Pharaoh. Yet, it was the hard times that have prepared me for this appointment. I could not have done it without Nefertekh or Amunebet — and especially without the Lord. This will be a new calling. It will take me away from my comfortable routines where the needed competencies have already been developed and make me stretch. Through stretching I grow.

He sat in the comfortable chair. A slave appeared with a tray of fruit and put it by his elbow. He absent-mindedly selected a fig and split it in half. As he chewed, his thoughts continued on the task which lay before him. Wanting to be alone with his thoughts, he dismissed the slaves.

He knelt by the bed and poured out his thanks. For a long time he knelt there offering his prayer of faith, prayer of love, and prayer of thanksgiving. When he finished, he remained on his knees. A sweet, peaceful feeling permeated his being. It was a feeling felt many times before — a feeling he knew prefaced the inside voice speaking to him. "My son, I am ever with you. You have been concerned about your father. Jacob lives and you will see him again in the flesh."

Tears streamed silently down Joseph's cheeks. It was the answer he sought.

Days became weeks while Joseph lived at the palace. Announcements of Joseph's appointment as grand vizier went to the far corners of Egypt. Court and temple officials planned a great festival celebrating the appointment. Barge loads of people floated down the Nile, jamming into the city of On for the celebration.

"Where are they all coming from?" Joseph asked the old vizier. The old man shook his head. "From as far away as Nubia. Barges come from every city. The soldiers at the gates tell me there are over five hundred thousand people in the city."

Morning of the festival arrived. At the palace, the great court glowed with torches. The procession would wind from the palace to the great temple. Chamberlains, servants, and slaves hurried this way and that, lining up litters and chariots in strict order of protocol. Joseph's litter was placed directly behind the Pharaoh's.

Streaks of red lighted the eastern sky as the royal parade started its journey toward the temple. People had arisen early, snatched their holiday garments, decked themselves with flowers, and hurried to the streets. All over the city doors burst open as more and more people streamed from houses into streets already filled with the masses of Egypt. Dust rose in clouds from hurrying feet, shoulders thrust against bare shoulders, black heads bobbed like ripples in a current as the jubilant crowd surged forward. Throngs choked cross streets and the avenue solidly from palace to temple. Many scrambled into trees, others headed for rooftops. Swaying and jostling, they craned their necks for glimpses of the royal procession. Odors of sweat, ointment, and crushed flowers rose from their straining bodies to mingle with drifting dust.

Soldiers lined the avenue, holding back the crowd. They wore their finest battle dress — helmets, course kilts, cuirasses of quilted leather marked with insignia of their rank; scarlet belts with daggers or battle hatchets thrust through them. Shields pressed against the crowd, javelins pierced the air.

The procession wound slowly through crowded streets. Temple priestesses led with castanets and sistrums, playing music and strewing flower petals along the way. Priestesses followed Pharaoh's honor guard carrying royal pennants — Falcon, Ibis, and Crocodile — fluttering high above them. Then came the Pharaoh, followed by Joseph, the royal consort, and palace royalty.

Joseph watched the people as his litter, carried on the shoulders of six strong slaves, passed them. The crowd seemed frenzied, hands lifted, palms out in adoration, ecstasy glittering in their eyes. A mighty chant swept along the crowd. "Hail to Pharaoh, Horus, Sacred Son! Hail to the Strong Bull!"

As Joseph's litter passed, people chanted, "Hail Adon. Glory to Pharaoh's right hand. Hail Psothom-Phanech!" Dust rose in filmy veils past his palanquin. People leaped and shouted in their excitement — a scene to be forever etched on Joseph's memory. As they neared the temple he heard fragments of singing and the occasional boom of a drum. Deep chanting of priests rose on the clear air, accompanied by jangling sistrums. Sound swelled in volume. As they entered the temple courtyard, slaves carefully set the litters down. Joseph stepped out and took in the scene before him.

The gilded four-sided obelisk of polished granite on its projecting foundation dominated the square. On the foundation itself, four white-robed trumpeters blew long, slender brazen horns to signal the arrival of Pharaoh. The temple, made of gilded bricks, glittered and glistened like gold as the sun rose. Joseph was in the temple of the sun!

Priests, dressed in stiffly starched kilts, leopard skins on their backs and tails dangling, poured out of the temple into the square. One stood out above all the rest. Joseph started. Potiphar! Now named Petephres: the Chief Priest! Standing before Petephres, Joseph noted the twinkle in those kindly eyes he remembered so well. The audience strained to hear the ceremony as the chief priest began. The ceremony, Joseph felt, had the solemnity of a funeral. The chief priest handed Joseph the forty rolls of the law. "These must always be spread open on your table to read," he intoned. "They tell you of the ways of justice for this people."

As a signal from Potiphar/Petephres, Pharaoh himself stepped forward to instruct the new grand vizier. He spoke. "It is an abomination of the gods to show partiality ..." He solemnly intoned the points of the law, ending with the injunction, "Thou shalt regard him who is known to thee like him who is unknown, and him who is near like unto him who is far."

As the ceremony continued, Joseph's eyes caught a motion in the crowd nearby. A girl. A girl he knew he had seen before. But where? She had waved or done something to catch his eye. Now she smiled — not broadly, but gently. All expression was in her eyes — great glowing dark eyes that squeezed up from the bottom with the smile. Her eyebrows were high and rounded. The fine nose, set above red, smiling lips, was tilted adorably. Joseph thought her pointed chin was perfect, as was her high forehead. Never had he seen such beauty. Her burnished, golden-red hair was brushed softly back from the front and wound in a high, loose coil covered, but not hidden, by a diaphanous veil.

He felt redness rising from his collar and turned back to the ceremony. But he could not resist looking at the girl again. He noticed her delicate ears, high but not prominent cheekbones. She had a pale complexion as if she had spent her life protected from the rays of the desert sun. The most striking feature about her, however, was her soulful gaze. It was direct and innocent. She looked fragile and Joseph desired to offer her his protection. He heard his name mentioned and focused his attention back to the ceremony. When he looked again, the girl had disappeared.

The festival was over. Joseph was grand vizier. He had power over all of Egypt. But now another feeling filled his heart. Joseph, for the first time in his life, suspected he might be in love.

Chapter 12: Grand Visier

Nowet Amun, chief city on the upper Nile was beautiful beyond description. Joseph, who thought On and Avaris grand in design, thrilled at the magnificence of the city's architecture. He strolled through temple precincts in the city center, among gardens, groves and waterways. The mirror image of the opulent temple, reflected in the glass-like surface of the sacred lakes, touched his artist eye. After his stroll, he stepped into his sedan chair for the trip back to the dock. He rode, immersed in thought. His bearers carried him through narrow streets, crooked, filthy, and ill-smelling. They passed along broad, tree-lined avenues in the wealthier part of town. Hundreds of pylons and gilded flagstaffs lined the great road of the ram-sphinx god Amon.

Nowet Amun was the southernmost city Joseph visited on his inspection tour of Egypt. Here, just like in every other city, he met with the Council of Elders, chose assistants to supervise the storage of grain, and inspected available storage facilities. Now he could return to Avaris where he could report to Pharaoh and do some planning. The Nile had begun to rise. Once more the season of flooding would be upon them. New storage facilities must be available by harvest time.

Joseph felt tired. He had been away from the palace for almost three months. The swinging motion of his carved and gilded sedan chair, carried on the shoulders of four tall youths wearing gold aprons, just about put him to sleep. When the youths set the chair down on the dock, Joseph wearily climbed out and walked aboard the waiting ship. To avoid the hot noon sun pouring down upon the deck, he sought the shade of the awning. Comfortably seated, he looked around.

All sorts of water craft filled the river. Huge barges, linked together and piled with blocks of granite, floated ponderously downstream. Delicate boats of noblemen swept past, high, curled prows shining with gild, oars flashing in the sunlight. A temple bark with purple sail floated by. Tiny fishing boats, hardly more than bundles of papyrus reeds, scurried here and there like many-legged waterbugs.

River traffic decreased as Joseph's ship sailed away from Nowet Amun. A wide and sparkling expanse of the river lay before them. Boat landings and clusters of houses gave way to green farmlands on either side of the river. He summoned his scribe. From a cupboard at his feet, the scribe pulled out several papyrus rolls. Carefully stroking the paper with his reed brush, he wrote as Joseph dictated. Joseph told him of the preparedness of Nowet Amun, names of those he selected to be in charge of the storage program, and also told of the reaction of the leaders he had visited.

He took the papyrus and read through what he had written, then glanced at similar reports for Abydos, Memphis, On, Avaris, and smaller cities of the Nile valley. The ship dipped and rocked as it crossed the wake of a passing ferry. Joseph, interrupted in his thought, glanced again at the passing scenery. He longed again for the comfort of his home. His home was still in the Pharaoh's palace, but his new estate home was being constructed on the outskirts of the City of On. He, himself, had approved the final plans. In his mind he pictured the estate. The house itself would stand on extensive grounds. A towered gateway opened to a tree-lined path leading to the inner courtyard. Painted columns on either side marked the path. A flight of shallow steps led from the courtyard to the door of the house. Above the door would be a stone lintel inscribed with his name in bold letters. From the porch one would go through a vestibule to the north loggia. A handsome reception room and a huge central hall dominated that wing.

Sitting rooms and guest rooms were located in the west loggia. Joseph's private quarters, on the east side, would include a sitting room and the main bedroom. Joseph shut his eyes and pictured the bedroom. His bed would stand in a niche on a raised dais. Next to his bedroom would be the bathroom with a slab where he could sit or lie while servants poured water over him. Beyond the bathroom was the toilet. Servants' quarters lined the outside wall next to the kitchen and garden. Plans for the garden especially pleased Joseph. There would be a formal pool and rows of trees and shrubs. The pool would be alive with goldfish and lily pads.

As the sun set, slaves appeared on deck to remove Joseph's flashing collar, armbands, and his rigidly starched kilt. A slave, standing behind him, slipped his dressing robe over his shoulders. Another knelt to put his feet into soft leather sandals. Darkness came quickly. As a youth in Canaan, Joseph enjoyed the softness of evenings between sundown and dark. Here, there was no soft twilight. Within minutes after the sun set over the desert it was completely dark.

Pharaoh had ensured that, on the royal bark, Joseph would have all the comforts of the palace. Now he lay in his hammock, suspended between two of the upright spars. He listened to the soft slap of the boat's prow against the water, feeling the whisper of the sails. He grimaced, suddenly forgetting water and sails. In addition to the government business he had conducted, he had also attempted to complete a personal goal. Thirteen years earlier, when his friend, Desir, had been sold in the slave market, he had vowed he would find her and have her released. In every city, he had instructed local governors to search every wine shop and public bar for the girl. She had not been found.

As the ship flew silently down the Nile, Joseph thought again of the other girl — the one he had seen during his investiture in On. He had seen her again on his inspection trip. It had been nighttime and dark around the temple. Torch light sparkled across the waters of the great river. Iridescent! Priests chanted monotonous refrains to their many gods, but suddenly Joseph heard them no more. On the fringe of the crowd stood the girl. In the light of the flickering torches she had a fragile look about her. She had looked at him with a most soulful gaze. Chanting ended, the priests turned to reenter the temple. Joseph looked where she had stood. She was gone, disappearing as if she were a goddess. He had determined to find out who she was. The moon, incredibly large, rose above the desert, casting a shimmering path across the river's waters. Joseph lay in his hammock, thinking of this strange girl. He slipped into a peaceful sleep, a smile on his face, a desire in his heart.

Back in Avaris, he busied himself with his staff of scribes. He established a room in the palace where they could work. There, he drafted the first of what would be many laws concerning the preservation of the coming harvest. dictating to his scribes, he prescribed a universal tax of one-fifth of every crop, without respect to person or status. Such tax would be delivered into the royal storehouses punctually and without notice. The proclamation also informed people of the construction of new grain bins and silos to hold the wheat.

Joseph hired laborers to be consigned to each major city. There they constructed storehouses and corn pits. Soon, wherever Joseph went, he saw skittle-shaped corn bins grouped closely together in the courts of the cities. Tops of the bins could be opened to receive corn and stout doors below could open to empty the corn into waiting baskets of those who would buy and use the corn. The workers built the bins and storehouses on platforms of pounded clay to protect them from dampness or mice. Joseph also assigned workers to find caves and underground pits for the storage of grain. These were cleaned, lined, and guarded.

Wherever Joseph went, surrounded by his Nubian and Syrian bodyguard, people greeted him with lifted hands and shouts of "Adon! Live a long life, O friend of Pharaoh." After his investiture, in addition to the signet ring already given him, Pharaoh had placed a particularly heavy gold necklace around his neck. Joseph felt it was this badge of his office the people honored rather than himself. He did not particularly like the adulation.

Living at the palace during the first year after his release from prison, Joseph spent much time with Pharaoh. They discussed plans for the Two Lands, but also spent time just talking. Joseph found that Amenhotep, the Pharaoh, was a lonely young man — protected from others by his godship. None of his subjects could touch him or converse with him on a personal basis. Joseph became a close friend as well as Pharaoh's advisor. One day, while discussing the purpose of life, Amenhotep bluntly interrupted their conversation. He said, "Joseph, it is important that you soon take a wife."

Joseph raised his eyes in astonishment.

Amenhotep continued. "There are many women who would desire to be one of your wives."

Joseph started to protest, then thought of the beautiful maiden at the temple of On.

Pharaoh held up his hand. "Listen to me. I am still your king. The building of your estate is almost completed. It would be unfitting to live there without a wife. I will personally select for you a maiden — a virgin maiden of the blood of the Hyksos." He smiled at Joseph. "I know it is important to you to marry a Semite."

Joseph bowed in meek acceptance. What could he do? Then a plan began to formulate in his mind. "My king, may I select a wife for myself?" Pharaoh nodded. A grin spread across the thin face of the youthful king. "Perhaps you have already picked someone?"

A redness crept up from Joseph's throat, giving away whatever it was he would have said. "Yes, my lord. I have seen a maiden at the temple of On."

"So be it. I hereby dispatch you to On to find your wife. Also, while there, you pay your respects to Petephres, your old master."

"I shall do so, my lord." Joseph turned to go.

"Hold," Pharaoh said. Joseph turned back. "One other thing. Have you selected an overseer for your estate?"

"Yes, my lord."

"Who might it be?"

"I ask you to relieve Amunebet from his duties at your royal prison and assign him as my overseer."

The request took Pharaoh by surprise. He sat, chin cupped in his hand, a thoughtful expression on his face. "Amunebet?"

"Yes, my lord."

"So be it. I will have the necessary papers prepared." He waved his hand, dismissing Joseph.

The royal bark stopped at the prison at Zawe-Re. Joseph leaped ashore, carrying the papyrus orders for Amunebet. Joseph found him in his office, with papyrus rolls stacked all over the desk before him. Amunebet jumped to his feet.

"Joseph, it is you. I thought you would have forgotten me by now." Joseph clasped his arm, then hugged Amunebet. "Never do I forget my friends."

Amunebet waved at the rolls on his desk. "Things have not been the same since you left. The help one gets nowadays . . .!" He stepped back, looking on Joseph. "But what of you? What is happening now that you are the grand vizier?"

Modestly, Joseph smiled. "I enjoy assisting the great Pharaoh in providing leadership for the Two lands." Then he looked seriously at Amunebet. "While I was your 'guest', you often talked of a desire to leave the prison."

Amunebet nodded, then glumly replied. "I will probably spend the rest of my life here shepherding prisoners for the king."

"Is that what you want?" Joseph asked seriously.

"You know it is not!" Amunebet stoutly replied. "There is nothing I desire more than to leave this foul place."

"Then you shall!" Joseph handed Amunebet the roll of papyrus. Amunebet read through the paper, glanced up at Joseph, then reread the orders. "Your overseer? The overseer of your estate?" he asked, his tone incredulous.

Joseph nodded.

Amunebet jumped forward, threw his arms around Joseph's neck and held him tightly. He stepped back, embarrassed over his emotionalism, then slapped his clenched fist to his chest in a salute. "I promise to serve you faithfully and well. You have but to ask."

Grinning broadly, Joseph replied. "I'm asking now. If we don't hurry, the ship will pull from shore without us. How long will it take you to pack?"

The rest of the journey to On was without incident. Joseph and Amunebet spent their time visiting and planning. Amunebet was anxious to see the estate, and so was Joseph.

The estate was just downriver from On. Joseph watched as the bark maneuvered slowly by a stretch of papyrus marsh below the east bank. Dozens of people streamed out from the walls to greet them, some scrambling into the muddy river to get nearer. The sail slithered down its mast, leaving the sky suddenly empty.

Joseph and Amunebet stepped ashore. They had to walk carefully to avoid servants prostrated before them. Amunebet stopped to admire the outer walls. Laid up of a double course of sun-dried bricks, they were plastered with mica sand and glittered like facets of a gemstone.

Servants followed them as they wandered through the new buildings and out into the garden with its blue, reflecting pool. Joseph watched with a half smile as Amunebet gawked and touched.

Joseph stopped in the great hall. He motioned to a servant. "Bring everyone here," he commanded. "The servants need to meet the overseer."

The room filled quickly. There were Nubian slaves, Egyptian servants, field hands, and the many others necessary to run the huge estate. The room became crowded. Others filled the doorways.

Joseph stood on a raised platform on one end of the great hall. He pulled Amunebet up beside him. "This is your new master and overseer. It is he whom you will obey."

Amunebet spoke. He told servants and slaves what he would expect of them. He spoke kindly, but firmly, leaving no room for misinterpretation. He ended with a challenge. "Your master, the grand vizier of Egypt, will soon bring to the estate his bride. You will have everything in readiness for her." Heads nodded, some bowed. He and Joseph finished giving instruction, then started back for the dock. Amunebet turned to Joseph. " I'll stay to prepare things for your wedding."

Joseph grabbed his hand. "No," he said, his voice unnaturally loud. He calmed himself and continued. "It is a new experience for me to approach a maiden about marriage. I need your support." Amunebet smiled.

Joseph knew why. *Here I am,* he thought, *second only in command to Pharaoh, and usually so sure of myself – and now appearing shy.* As soon as they were on board, the captain cast off the lines. The crew raised the sleek, purple sail and they were again on their way. Distance was short, but the current was strong and the wind weak. The pilot sat on the slanting beak in the stern of the boat and operated the rudder with the perpendicular lever. A crewman at the goose-head in the prow tested the channel with a pole. Wind, freshened from the north, filled the sail. The keel cut smoothly through the water.

This was an important day for Joseph. Gentle rocking and gliding on the wide river put him in a reflective mood. He looked as pillared halls on the banks as they swept by. There were palm groves and green orchards; small villages with high dove-cotes, then the walls and glittering obelisk of On itself.

Chapter 13: Aseneth

Petephres' servant, a fat-bellied man in woven sandals and a knee-length linen apron, greeted them at the dock. Multi-colored ribbons, in which he had piously tied many knots, adorned his arms and back. His good-natured face was clean-shaven, framed by short, smooth hair on his round pate. At the temple, he ushered Joseph and Amunebet into Petephres' office. Joseph marveled at how much Potiphar had aged in the years since he had stood accused before him. Petephres had a round, full face. With age and soft living, his skin had become wrinkled, yellowed and wizened. Sparse hair had turned totally gray.

He rose from his seat as Joseph and Amunebet entered, thrusting forth his hand in greeting. "A long life to you, my friend."

"And to you, Great High Priest of On," replied Joseph. He motioned towards Amunebet. "You remember Amunebet, governor of Pharaoh's prison, now my friend and overseer."

Petephres nodded and motioned them to a bench along the wall. When they were comfortably seated, he looked inquiringly at Joseph. "And what brings you to the temple?"

Joseph looked at Amunebet and cleared his throat, finally blurting out, "I am come to seek a wife."

Smiling, Petephres relaxed. "A wife? In the temple? Any particular one? You may choose any or all."

Joseph shook his head. "No, I only have desire for one. I have seen her here several times. She is the one I would marry."

Petephres stepped to the door and clapped his hands. A servant appeared. Petephres whispered in his ear. Moments later, a large lady dressed in temple robes entered. "This is Henhenet, chief priestess of the temple. Tell her whom you want."

Joseph looked at the chief priestess. Though high colored, she suggested austerity. Her gray eyes reminded him of the underside of olive leaves, her nose a hawk's. Her demeanor suggested directness, one who would not blink at the unexpected. "I desire a maiden from the temple to take as my wife."

She raised her eyebrows.

"There is one, about sixteen," Joseph continued. "Dark eyes and red hair. I would like to see her."

Petephres started, then looked at Henhenet. "I think I know the girl you seek," he said. He nodded to Henhenet. "Bring Asenath." When she returned, Henhenet had a young lady in tow. It was she! For a moment Joseph averted his eyes, then he looked at her. She was just as he remembered, only much more beautiful up close. Her eyes, which held his attention before, glowed large and luminous from a pale face. Her hair, hanging in two long braids down her back, was golden-red and filmy. Her forehead was not broad but her cheekbones were remarkably wide and high. She stood boldly looking at him. Her remarkable eyes held steady, unshifting, on his face.

Petephres motioned her forward, then put his arm around her waist. Turning to Joseph, he said, "Joseph, meet my daughter, Asenath." Joseph stepped back. Potiphar's daughter? Then he remembered the twelve-year old girl walking sedately toward the women's quarters at the estate, the girl in the doorway at his trial before Potiphar. So that is why I felt I knew her. His heart beat with pleasure. Heat rushed to his cheeks. Still speechless, he looked at her again. Her breast rose and fell with her emotion. A faint flush stained the ivory above her cheekbones. Graciously Petephres spoke. His face showed no emotion. He was solemn; a statesman. "Look upon her, my son. Is she not fair?"

Joseph breathed deeply. He looked aside for an instant while he uttered a prayer, then spoke. "Great and noble Petephres, she is more fair than any person I have ever looked upon. With your permission, I would take her for my wife."

Asenath's nostrils flared with her quick intake of breath. Joseph could see his statement had not displeased her. Her eyes seemed to bore into him, her shoulders rising and falling with each breath. The world was still as Joseph waited for Petephres' answer.

Knowing he would be well-rewarded by Pharaoh's grand vizier, Petephres smiled. With an eloquent gesture, he said, "Asenath shall be your bride. We shall make the necessary arrangements."

Joseph bowed formally. He made no secret of his admiration, but it would not be proper to appear too anxious. "Please make your arrangements through my overseer, Amunebet."

The visit ended. Joseph had accomplished his purpose. He looked again at Asenath. Her lips parted as though in eager expectancy. Her eyes still probed his.

Henhenet grasped Asenath by her elbow, wheeled her around, and they were gone. The room suddenly seemed empty, as if the torch had been snuffed out.

Petephres sat and folded his hands. He leaned forward, torchlight flashing off the gems on his fingers, reflecting pinpoints of light. He thoughtfully regarded Joseph. "How soon the wedding?"

"Your daughter will need time for her preparations," Joseph replied. "The flooding of the Nile will be in three weeks. May the wedding take place during the new year celebrations?"

Petephres nodded. Done! Joseph bowed again to this man who had been his master and now held the office of Chief Priest of Osiris.

On the trip back to the estate, Joseph was insouciant. He thought, *Never have I been so happy. The Lord truly directs my path.* Athyr, the closing month of the old year, passed ever so slowly as Egypt and Joseph prepared for a royal wedding.

Asenath, her four personal maids, and her mother came by boat from On for her marriage to Joseph. Pharaoh, himself, came from Avaris. Petephres and his priests came from On in a separate boat. Several score musicians and dancers enlivened the celebration. Joseph hired mourners to wail and beat their breasts as a sign that the maiden in Asenath would now be dead.

Joseph, clean-shaven and light-hearted, dressed in a long-sleeved, white linen robe. A servant carefully placed the gold chain and amulet which Pharaoh had presented to him around his neck. Pharaoh's signet ring circled his finger. Of all the dignitaries, he was the only one bareheaded.

In preparation for the wedding, the estate, under Amunebet's close supervision, received another coat of whitewash. Gravel walks were freshly raked, furniture dusted and shined. Everything sparkled. Pharaoh and his wife, the queen, Kemsiyet, sat on the dais in throne chairs watching the dancing. Performers swirled and swayed to music of cymbals and tambourines. Joseph remained totally unconscious of the dancers. His eyes seldom left Asenath. She stood to one side, surrounded by her maids. Though but sixteen, she stood tall and beautiful and nicely developed. Joseph smiled. Her eyes had been lengthened by makeup and her lips were tinted a berry red. A blue-black wig hung below her shoulders. *I prefer her real hair, and without so much makeup,* he thought.

The entertainment seemed endless to him, but finally the time came for the exchange of wedding vows. Joseph and Asenath walked forward and knelt before Pharaoh. They clasped hands across his knees, careful not to touch the untouchable king. They looked at each other, eyes locked. At the appropriate places in the ceremony, they repeated the vows uttered by Pharaoh.

Pharaoh and Kemsiyet led the procession to begin the feast. The wedding dinner started with fresh wine from the vineyards and small squares of baked fish simmered in olive oil. The main course was duck braised with lotus root, fresh vegetables from the garden, and freshly-baked breads. Servants cleared away the duck, changed plates, and brought trays heaped with fresh fruit and cake. Date wine followed, poured in goblets blue as Egypt's sky.

Guests lingered over the food. Finally, the procession formed once more. With myrtle strewn in their path, the newlyweds proceeded to the bridal chambers where they were put to bed among fresh flowers and fine linen. The lesser priests of On stood outside their door, chanting the prescribed sayings. Inside the bridal chamber, Joseph cupped Asenath's chin in his hand and gently kissed her. Then he pulled her against him with a sudden passion.

Tybi, the month of flooding, passed. Now the waters of the Nile receded daily. Joseph, returning to his duties, traveled down the Nile. As usual, he stationed himself at the highest point of the poop deck near the great stern sweep. He watched the inundated land slowly unwind like a scroll before him. Brown fields glistened with their covering of water, lending contrast to the saffron desert behind and the blue sky above. He was thankful for his pilot. With the river over its banks, he was not sure he could have found the main channel, though it was dotted on either side with spindly palms thrusting their heads into the sky.

On the smooth water a flotilla of boats, topped by monstrous sails on swaying masts, passed on their way upriver. Joseph idly wondered if it were part of the Phoenician fleet on its way to Memphis. Noticing the sporadic and ragged wind, Joseph commented to the captain, "The wind is not very favorable for sailing."

As he pulled on the large beam which controlled the rudder, the captain replied, "No wind is favorable for a ship that does not know its destination."

Joseph nodded. That was a philosophy he certainly believed. One must have goals to be successful. His thoughts came back to the purpose of his journey. This was the first year of the seven years of plenty. His main warehouses and storage bins were ready for the input of grain and corn. He had a difficult time keeping his mind on the task. He missed Asenath, but today his heart was especially full.

Before he left the estate, Asenath had called him to her. Already he felt a loneliness, leaving her for the first time. Apparently she had similar feelings. She held his hand as they walked to the kiosk near the garden.

They sat silently, watching goldfish swim in the clear water of the pond. She turned her eyes to him, eyes that always seemed to melt him.

"Is it necessary, my husband, that you leave at this time?"

"It is something I must do. My staff in Avaris meets today to plan for collection of taxes and storage of crops. Besides, Pharaoh himself has asked that I come to Avaris for a progress report." He looked at her and squeezed her hand. "I will only be gone a week." He smiled at her solemn demeanor.

Unexpectedly, she smiled back, then leaned toward him with a confidential air. "My dear," she murmured in his ear, "Would it hasten your return to me if I told you we are going to have a baby?" He looked at her, incredulously. "A baby?" His voice broke. "She laughed at his response. "Yes, my dear, a baby." He pulled her close. A baby. Jacob would have a grandchild through his loins.

Her words made it much more difficult to leave. Now, he wished he could turn the boat around and hurry back to Asenath. But no. He must also be about Pharaoh's business. However, as soon as... He left the thought dangling. Perhaps in Avaris he could choose some trinkets for Asenath. Then he began to worry. Should Asenath have extra maids to care for her? What about a midwife? And a nursery? Would they need a maid to care for the infant?

When they arrived at Avaris, the ship bumped gently against the landing. As soon as ropes secured it to the dock, Joseph stepped ashore. The crowd, waiting to greet him, shouted their acclamations. "Psothom-Phanech!" Psothom-Phanech!" Gold-decked dignitaries stepped forward. Great plumed fans shaded the gangplank. It was a greeting such as Pharaoh himself might expect.

After a day with his assistants, planning collection of taxes and storage processes for grain and corn, Joseph made his way to the palace. It would be a pleasure to visit the young king once more. It had been several months since Pharaoh had presided at his and Asenath's wedding. Amenhotep sat in his reception hall. Apparently this had been the day for him to arbitrate the affairs of his people. Several groups of citizens left the hall as Joseph entered. One group had yet to be heard. Joseph stayed in the background, observing. He watched the dipping of snowy headcloths and ink-black wigs. He heard the murmur of ceremonious greetings and the scuffling of sandals. Slaves stationed around the hall moved the stagnant air with huge, plumy fans.

He was pleased to see Queen Kemsiyet again. The first time he had seen her up close was at his wedding. He smiled as he thought that on that night his mind had been on other things. As he waited now, he studied the queen. Her nose had a fine, almost arrogant arch, well set off by the delicacy of jawline and nostril. Her whole face held an elusive charm. Wide dark eyes, now lengthened by paints, appeared impenetrable under high, arched eyebrows. She had a frozen half-smile on full, reddened lips. It was as if the smile, too, were painted on. She wore a dress of white linen with a necklace of blue-green turquoise stones set with gold nuggets. Today she wore a blue wig, hair cascading down in ringlets framing and softening her high, unwrinkled forehead.

The scribe's voice droned to a halt at last, then it was Joseph's turn.

He stepped forward, and dropped to one knee before the royal couple. Pharaoh smiled tiredly. "Come, my friend. Let us go to the garden. We have much to discuss." He helped Queen Kemsiyet from the dais and whispered in her ear. She smiled and left the hall.

"Is Asenath well?" Pharaoh asked as they walked to the garden.

"She is expecting our first child," Joseph said, the sound of the words pleasing him.

Amenhotep clapped his hands in delight. "An heir!"

"More than an heir," Joseph said quietly. "A continuation of God's covenant with my great-grandfather, Abraham."

They sat on a bench by the pool under the shade of the tamarisk tree. It was a place Joseph had often sat. It had a familiar and friendly feel. Pharaoh asked, "How are your plans for this year of plenty?"

Joseph stood and paced as he talked. "My king, I have hired the most capable assistants in the land. They are honest. They will manage well. I have delegated much responsibility to them."

"Pharaoh nodded. "That is well. What of storage facilities?"

"In each city we have built new granaries and new warehouses. They will easily hold not only this year's crop, but crops from several years to come. After this year's harvest, we will evaluate our storage capacity and decide how many more facilities we need to build."

Again Pharaoh nodded. "I am pleased." He waved his hand as if to dismiss the subject. "Enough of that. Tell me about yourself. Are you happy?"

"Happier than I have ever been," Joseph said, sitting beside the king. "Not only because I have a beautiful wife and an expected baby; not even because you have given me power and responsibility. It is more than that. Many years ago I promised my God that I would serve wherever I was placed. Now, through your trust in me, I have the opportunity to serve your entire people."

"You believe strongly in that, don't you?"

Joseph nodded. "I think that serving others is the only way to be truly happy." Nervously he stood again, pacing near the pool. As he passed the tamarisk tree, he dragged his hand over the heavy bark, feeling its serrations.

Pharaoh's smile faded into thoughtfulness. "If only that were a philosophy of all mankind. Where did you learn such a philosophy? Certainly, not as a slave."

Before he answered, Joseph again rubbed his hands on the tree's rough bark. "My king, as a youth I took no thought for the future. I just supposed it would take care of itself. So begging your pardon, my king, it was as a slave that I developed that philosophy. I learned to serve where I was put, doing the very best I could in each situation. I knew an accounting must be kept in the heavens, so that, if I gave willingly, there would have to be a return." He walked over to the Pharaoh. "None of us know the circumstances in which we will be placed. But man has to have hope. Without a hope for the future, there is no power in the present."

"Well said, my philosopher friend." Pharaoh stood, extending a hand to Joseph. "I am a better king because of you. I know you are anxious to be home with your wife. So go to her, my friend. I will see you again at the time of planting."

Joseph bowed, then hurried from the garden. The sun lay golden on the western horizon by the time his litter arrived back at the dock. As soon as Joseph was on board sailors loosed the lines. He watched sailors pull the sail up the mast. Rib by rib it rose like a gigantic fin — a great wing unfolding in the evening twilight. The setting sun turned it gold. The sail was a majestic sight. To Joseph it seemed almost alive — as if the cluster of straining bodies on the deck below had nothing to do with its spreading. The sail caught the wind from the north, and the bark headed for the channel's center.

Within three months, the Nile had receded back within its banks, brown in its bed and in isolated pools in the fields. Land emerged anew. Before the ground was dry, farmers sowed seeds in their fields. Under heat of the Egyptian sun, crops seemed almost to pop out of the ground. One day the fields looked brown, the next, green.

Long rites at the temple of On began at the time of the highest inundation of the Nile. Incense still smoldered on altars as prayers and incantations of leopard-skin robed priests droned on. Each night priestesses paraded to the water's edge to scatter flower petals to Mother Nile. Their dancing, accompanied by rattle of sistrums and jingle of tambourines, was a fitting accompaniment for the priests' prayers for a good harvest.

Joseph spent his time planning for the years of famine, but without neglecting his now obviously pregnant wife. Only a few days had passed since Asenath had first felt life within her. Joseph stayed close, never leaving the estate.

During the time he awaited her delivery, Joseph fulfilled one of his childhood dreams. He sent Amunebet to Memphis to the horse auction. He had given specific instructions as to what to purchase. Now he anxiously awaited Amunebet's return. From afar, he spotted the royal bark sailing down the Nile. He ran to the dock. As the ship drew closer, he could see that Amunebet had been successful. Loaded on board were not one, but two beautiful white stallions — white horses with pink noses, pink eyes, and pink ears. As they were unloaded, he ran his hands down their sides. They were the most beautiful horses he had ever seen. They pranced around the dock, heads and tails held high. Amunebet and his helper had a difficult time holding them.

Amunebet smiled broadly. "I have another surprise for you." He nodded to a sailor, who led a woman of about thirty off the boat.

Joseph looked at her quizzically. She looked familiar.

Abruptly, she prostrated herself at his feet and stretched out her hands to him.

He looked at Amunebet.

Amunebet shrugged. "The governor of Memphis said it was someone you wanted. Someone by the name of Dayseer, or something like that."

Joseph inhaled quickly. Could it be! He reached down and pulled the woman to her feet. Looking into her eyes he knew it was so. He had fulfilled the promise he made to himself over thirteen years before. He spoke kindly to her. "Is it really you, Desir?"

She nodded mutely. Tears brimmed in her eyes.

He put his arm around her, turned and walked to the estate. "You will be set free."

Desir finally found her voice. "Yes, master. But where shall I live? Where shall I go?"

Joseph turned to her. "I am not your master, but your friend." He motioned toward the estate. "This is my home. You will live here as long as you desire."

A tremor went through her body. They walked on through the gate. Desir looked at him, a question in her hollow eyes.

"You will feel better after a bath and with new clothes. Remember, you will be a free woman as soon as I can draw up the papers. This will be your home." Joseph turned Desir over to one of the maids to be bathed and given a new wardrobe.

He hurried to the stables. Several servants brushed down the white stallions. He personally fed them grain. He felt a great satisfaction. Two dreams come true in one day, he exulted. But now I have one more goal.

Next day he watched as the stable boy harnessed the stallions to his chariot. They pranced in the harness, eyes white and nostrils dilated. With exception of several trial runs under Pharaoh's direction, he had never driven horses. He had ridden somewhat in his childhood, but even there horses had been reserved for grown-ups. Now he stepped in the chariot, signaled the slave, and away they went. In a few minutes he came limping back to the stable. Amunebet withheld his smile, merely sending the stable boy to find the horses and chariot and bring them back.

Joseph did not give up. Each day he doggedly stepped into the chariot. He found that handling a chariot and a wild team of horses took infinite patience and skill. Each day he improved, though during the first few weeks he limped home more times than he rode.

"I dread each hour you are away from me," Asenath told Joseph. He hugged her, reaching over her large stomach. "Everything will be all right," he said. "Every day I learn more about handling the horses. Just a few more days."

"I am frightened that you will leave me a widow with a child to raise," she pleaded.

As the days of her confinement drew close, she resented more and more Joseph's being away from her. Hours dragged as she awaited his return. As she stood on the balcony one day, looking into the desert, hands shading her eyes, a sharp pain made her gasp. Then another. Oh, it is time, she thought, and Joseph is not here. The sun sank, the glory of the sky fading as her pains increased in intensity. Still no Joseph. The earth became shrouded in darkness. Soon the moon, incredibly large, rose over the desert. Her pains forced her to her bed, where she lay under the watchful eye of Desir and the two midwives Joseph had hired.

Her pains seemed magnified because Joseph was not there. One maid bathed her forehead in cool water while the other fetched hot water. Desir sat beside Asenath and held her hands, whispering comforting words. Just when she thought she could bear it no longer, Joseph rushed in. Desir jumped up as he moved quickly to Asenath's side and took her clammy hand. He stroked her hair, whispering calming words.

Asenath smiled in relief. Labor would not be nearly so bad now that the man she loved sat beside her.

At the time of delivery, the midwife hurried Joseph from the room. Nervously, he paced the floor of the great hall. He could not help but think of when his mother had died in childbirth. "Father, protect my wife and child," he prayed aloud.

A cry came from the women's quarters, a lusty cry of release and of anger. He rushed back into the bedroom. A baby, bloodied and red lay face-down on Asenath's stomach, while the midwife busily cut the cord and bandaged the navel. Joseph sat down and looked at Asenath's face. She lay with eyes closed, her breathing even.

The midwife cleaned and wrapped the baby in soft cotton cloths, then handed the small bundle to Joseph. A boy! He looked upon its fresh profile.

Asenath spoke from the bed. "His nose shows a hint of jutting strength." Joseph laughed. "And his softly-curved cheeks and full lips bespeak gentleness."

She held out her arms for the baby.

Joseph tenderly placed him in her arms. He wondered, What will the future bring for this firstborn son. What will the boy be like? Will the man he will become be a man of strength, or of weakness? Of cruelty, or of gentleness? Joseph looked again at his new son, then asked himself, How can I help mold this son of God?

Asenath broke into his thoughts. "Why do you look so sad?"

Joseph smiled. "I thought of my father, and how he might never know this grandson."

She clucked her tongue. "Have you not told me that your God promised you that you would see your father again in the flesh?

He chuckled. "Thank you for calling me to repentance. I will not doubt again."

When the baby was eight days of age, Joseph circumcised him. "Why do you do that?" Asenath asked, wincing at the baby's screams. "It is a symbolic act to remind us of the covenant the Lord made with my great-grandfather, Abraham."

That night Joseph inscribed a new entry on the bronze plates. "Our first son is born. I have named him Manasseh. Through him, God has made me forget all my toil."

Chapter 14: From Plenty to Famine

For four years the Nile gave bounteously of itself. Each year's harvest seemed better than the last. Grain bins filled to overflowing. Additional warehouses and grain bins were under construction to handle the surplus. Fields were not the only fruitful things. Asenath conceived again and she and Joseph now expected their second child. Manasseh, a precocious child, bright for his age, gave Joseph great joy.

Joseph, after numerous spills and bruises, mastered the art of driving a chariot. With exception of the team of Pharaoh, his spirited albino stallions surpassed all other teams in the land, both in speed and beauty. Joseph loved to grasp the reins, to feel the surge and nervous strength of the horses as they charged down one of the many roads across the desert vastness.

The day after Desir arrived on the estate, Joseph instructed his chief scribe to issue her papers of manumission. Signing it, he fulfilled his promise. Desir was no longer a slave. She wanted to remain on the estate to serve Asenath, which he permitted. From the beginning, Joseph noticed a bond between Amunebet and Desir. He smiled now as he thought back on the almost awkward courtship of Amunebet, who had never married, and Desir, who had been a slave for so long. Joseph culminated the closing of the second year of plenty by performing a ceremony uniting them in marriage. Now, they had a son of their own. The boy, Tem, well-muscled and sturdy like his father, was the apple of Amunebet's eye. They were rarely separated.

Joseph sat with Amunebet in the cool shade of his garden kiosk. Manasseh, four years of age, and Tem, one, played at their feet. From where he sat, Joseph could see acres of fields under cultivation: orchards, vineyards, and gardens. Behind him lay his house and outbuildings. Somewhere inside was the woman he loved. He cleared his throat. "It seems to me," he said, " that God has blessed me with everything my heart desired except for one thing."

Amunebet nodded, "And what is that?"

"I would like to see my father before he dies, and my brother, Benjamin." He closed his eyes. "It has been eighteen years since I last saw my father. I wonder if he still lives."

Seeing Joseph's introspective mood, Amunebet excused himself. "I must take care of the vineyard."

After he left, Joseph continued his meditation. To himself he asked: *What has happened to Benjamin. What of my other brothers?* Joseph uttered a silent prayer. *Please God, let our family be together once again.* He pulled the leather bag from his neck, opened the drawstring and dropped the smooth pebble into his palm. He had many possessions, but no material thing seemed as valuable to him as this small, smooth stone. His reverie was interrupted by a tug on his skirt.

"Father."

He put the stone away, then lifted Manasseh to his lap. "What is it, son?"

Manasseh's young forehead was wrinkled, his face troubled. "Father, why can't we have many gods like my friends?"

It was a question Joseph had anticipated. He had known that, as soon as Manasseh was old enough, he would want to know why he had different beliefs than the other children. Though Asenath was of Semitic origins, being descended from the Hyksos who had invaded Egypt two hundred years before, she had resisted converting to the idea of one God. The Hyksos had adopted Egyptian customs, including their many gods. Her further complication was having the high priest of On as her father. Patiently Joseph taught her. She now accepted and worshipped El Shaddai with him. Joseph looked at his son. "Manasseh," he began, "though we live in Egypt, we are not Egyptians."

The boy cocked his head, a questioning look in his eyes.

"Egyptians worship many gods, as you know. Osiris, Horus, Re, Atem and Amon — all of whom are gods of the sun. Then there is Anubis, the jackal-headed god of the afterworld, Bast, the cat god, Mut the buzzard god, Mestert the cow god, Sekhmet the lion god, Ptah, the fire god, and Uachet of Buto — the serpent god. In fact, my son, there seems to be a god for everything: tribal gods, village gods, folk gods that protect against illness and evil spirits: a cobra goddess, a falcon god, a donkey god, a jackal god, even a baboon and a crocodile god."

He could not tell whether Manasseh understood all he told him, but the child continued to look into Joseph's eyes with an expression of trust. "Our belief goes back many years, my son. The One God spoke to your great, great, grandfather Abraham when he lived here in Egypt. God told him He had heard his prayers and would bless him. He told Abraham He would be his God and would lead him to the promised land. God promised Abraham He would make of him a great nation and would bless him above measure and make his name great among all nations. He also promised Abraham that through his seed, all the families of the earth would be blessed." Pulling Manasseh close, Joseph continued. "My son, you are part of that seed — part of that blessing. The One God told me He brought me to Egypt to fulfill the promise made to Abraham. You are part of the promise."

"Father, will we ever see grandfather?"

"The Lord said so, my son. We must trust the Lord."

Manasseh still seemed confused. Joseph realized it was a lot for a four-year-old to absorb. Manasseh climbed down from his father's lap, then looked up into Joseph's eyes. "Father, is the One God our God and no one else's?"

Joseph smiled. "No, son. He is everyone's God. The problem is that few yet know Him. Through us, the whole earth will get to know Him, and thus will be blessed."

Manasseh had one more question. Looking very serious, he asked, "Is the One God mean like Ptah?"

"No, son. The One God is a loving God. He is not like a bull who runs in the fields, nor is He like the crocodile who would eat you. He isn't even like the sun which warms the earth, but has no feeling. He is a loving Father who wants our happiness and who will help us all he can if we will but give Him opportunity to do so."

Satisfied, Manasseh turned back to his play. But Joseph sat thinking of what he had said. *How can I teach my children to follow the One God when there are so many other influences pulling them?*

Asenath's second delivery was easier than the first. Desir never left her side from the time of her first pain. The midwife was with her for only an hour when Joseph heard the squalling of the newborn child. He hurried into the room. The midwife already had the baby cleaned and rubbed with olive oil. Desir stood by the bed, wrapping the baby in soft, clean linen. The midwife said, "It is a boy."

Joseph raised his eyes to the heavens. "Thank you, Lord." He turned back to the baby, gently taking it from Desir's arms. Eyes in the red, wrinkled face remained tightly closed, the fists clenched. Joseph teased a finger out from the fist, so tiny, yet perfectly formed. Once again he thrilled at the process of birth — of creation. Yes, even co-creation with God — an awesome thought. Still holding the baby he turned to his wife. Beads of sweat still stood on Asenath's forehead. Although pale, she smiled wanly at him. Joseph leaned over and kissed her gently. There seemed no need for words.

The midwife finished her cleanup and stood waiting at the door. She motioned to Joseph. He joined her. She looked troubled. "The little one," she said. "His foot . . ."

Joseph looked at her curiously. "What is it?"

She nodded her head towards the baby. "The baby's foot is crooked. He is imperfect and should be cast into the mouth of Ptah." Joseph looked shocked. "No!" He shook his head and motioned her out of the room. The maids and Desir followed. He moved to Asenath's side, again taking her hand.

She looked at him. "What is it?"

"Nothing, my dear one."

Asenath whispered. "Please give him to me."

He put the infant in the crook of her arm. She smiled as she looked into the tiny red face, caressing the baby's cheeks with her fingertips. "He is so beautiful."

Joseph nodded.

"He looks like you."

Shrugging, Joseph said, "He should. He is my son."

"What will you name him?"

"I shall call him Ephraim."

"What does it mean?"

"In the language of my fathers, it means God has caused me to be fruitful in the land of my affliction."

"Is this really the land of your affliction?"

"It was until I met you."

"Are you happy, my Joseph?"

"Happier than you can know," he replied, smiling.

Two more years of plenty quickly passed. Each year the river rose on schedule and blessed the land. Harvests remained plentiful, grain bins full. Ephraim, though he walked and ran with a limp, did not let his crippled foot slow him down. Asenath could not understand how he got into so many things. He was so busy! Manasseh had been such a quiet child. Now here was Ephraim. He was continually asking questions, getting into things, running here and there, teasing Manasseh, and exasperating his mother. She shook her head and smiled. "He is not mischievous," she said, "just curious and eager to learn."

Pharaoh had also become a father. He had an heir. Friendship between Joseph and Pharaoh deepened to become a warm and intimate bond. Each time they talked they delved deeper into the meaning of life.

For seven years winds and waters had provided the annual flood of the Nile. Harvests had been rich. People praised both Pharaoh and

Joseph. Now the eighth year had come. Spring wore on, but instead of rising, the river shrank between its banks as the heat of the land grew more intense. It was the first year since Joseph came to Egypt that the Nile failed to rise. For forty days the burning khamsin winds blew out of the Nubian wastelands, their hot breath drying out stubbled fields. Winds filled the air with swirls of sand, stinging sweating backs and squinted eyes of those who dared venture outside. Almost without cease, winds blew all summer and throughout harvest time. Sun burned down, gathering intensity, shining mercilessly. Heat waves rose from parched and lifeless fields. A heat-soaked silence lay over the brooding and dwindling river valley.

Near the river, great cracks in the dry mud spread crazily in all directions, wide enough to trip a full-grown kine, deeper in places than a man's staff. Soil, once rich, became powdery like desert sand. A burning stillness settled over the land. Feeble attempts to irrigate with the shadoof failed. Plants that did come up through the soil soon wilted and died. Winds filled the air with dust and sand that choked growth until even trees stretched leafless trunks and arms into the sky.

Non-agricultural business of Egypt died with the soil. Without a river to provide transportation, alabaster, granite, and basalt quarries closed. Importation of cedar trees from Phoenicia halted. Through it all, selling of grain prospered. Superintended by a staff of a thousand scribes under Joseph's direction, the business boomed. People, though warned during the seven fat years, had put the seven lean years out of their minds. Now came the day of reckoning. No person had enough grain stored. Farmers, weavers, and sandalmakers grew thinner. Living at all became difficult for the people who dwelt along what had been the long green ribbon of the Nile.

Some remembered when the Nile had failed to rise for one year, so they remained complacent, knowing it had never failed two years in a row. When dry winds continued into the second year and the Nile shrank even more, tension mounted. People watched waters dwindle day after day. With exception of very small boats, all navigation ceased. Wharfs and docks rose tall and stark above curling mud. Sand bars were now islands high above the water level. The price of grain climbed. Those rich enough paid for grain with silver and gold. Joseph, however, let no one go hungry. When the poor cried to him, he distributed grain from the stores without cost.

In Canaan, famine hit hard and fast. No extensive rivers flowed through Canaan — only the brief, shallow Jordan. It barely watered its own thin valley and could not reach beyond the range of hills that pressed closely upon it. Plants depended upon dew, mountain springs and rain. Now, there was no dew and no rain. Each day springs became smaller. Water in the well near Israel's encampment dropped lower, requiring a long rope to reach it. Simeon and the other sons of Jacob had never seen a drouth like this. Burning day followed burning day. Cattle and sheep, ribs showing through scrawny hides, picked at low leaves of scrub brush and the occasional wild grass they could find in the hard, reddish earth. Flies and gnats plagued the land. Every day the sun rose and fell in a cloudless blue sky. In Israel's camp, hunger became common. If that were not bad enough, streams of travelers passed through Hebron on their way to Egypt. The caravans stirred up clouds of dust which settled on what living vegetation survived, turning it gray and choking it.

Even Joseph's estate felt the famine. Previously, there had been an abundance of water — a lotus pond in the pleasure garden, a well for drinking water, square basins sunk in the ground among orchards and vegetable gardens. Most were now dry. His crops withered, like everyone else's, but Joseph felt secure. Grain filled his bins. Joseph doubled the size of guard units at border gates to regulate the flow of those coming into Egypt. Guards recorded the name of each person coming through the border. Everyone entering the land filled out a census form. He required records to be precise. People listed their names, trades, and places of origin. The census also required names of fathers and grandfathers. Each night a fast runner brought to Joseph the lists of those who had passed through the border. He pored over the lists, reading them carefully from beginning to end, looking for certain names.

Jacob, now 128 years of age, had used up all alternatives for his extensive family. There was nothing else to do. He called his sons to his tent. There is grain in Egypt. You must go there and buy grain for our people. Otherwise, we starve."

Napthali asked, "Who will go?"

Jacob looked around at the faces of his eleven sons. Benjamin sat next to him on his right. "All will go except Benjamin. Take donkeys loaded with gifts for the Pharaoh and to bring back grain."

Joseph worked hard. It had not been easy to oversee a country squeezed by famine. But despite his hard work and heavy burden of cares for the needs of the people, he remained in high spirits. It became a matter of coping with confidence. Each day he wrote in his journal.

Occasionally, he deemed something important enough to inscribe onto the brass plates. One day, after perusing the list of border crossers, he ran from the house waving a roll of papyrus. "Amunebet, they have come."

The overseer ran from his office. "What is it? Has something happened?" "My brothers. They passed through the border guards."

"All eleven of them?"

"No. The name of Benjamin is not on the list." He reflected briefly. "But that is a good sign. It probably means my father lives and keeps Benjamin with him."

He gave the list to Amunebet. "Bring these men to the estate. I will receive them here."

"Will they recognize you?"

He shook his head.

"Will you recognize them?"

There was no hesitation on Joseph's part. "Yes. Though it has been almost twenty-three years, I will recognize them." He smiled as he thought of the huge Simeon and the lanky Reuben.

"Will you speak to them in their tongue, or Egyptian?"

Joseph clapped a hand on Amunebet's shoulder. "Good reminder. It would be improper to speak in their tongue. They might immediately recognize me and that I do not want. No, I will speak in Egyptian. Make sure the interpreter, Hotpe, is here."

"If I may ask, Master Joseph, why don't you want them to recognize you? They are your brothers."

Joseph frowned. "I intend to test them to find out if they have any sorrow or repentance for selling me as a slave. I also want to determine the status of my father and Benjamin before my brothers find out who I am." He looked around solemnly. "I shall learn all that has happened." He slapped his fist into his hand. "I must also find a way to get Benjamin and my father here."

Amunebet nodded his understanding.

Joseph continued. "My brothers tore my coat, threw me into a pit, sold me as a slave. Now they have to stand before me. That is justice."

"Will you exact punishment upon them?"

Joseph shook his head. "No. They have probably been punished enough, just seeing my father's sorrow. I do not seek revenge. I forgave them long ago"

"Forgiveness could not have been easy."

Joseph reflected for a moment. "It never is. But I have learned forgiveness must be instantaneous. Otherwise, only he who is unforgiving suffers."

Amunebet looked puzzled, but shrugged.

Joseph, still thinking about the question, added, " Besides, it was not they who sent me to Egypt, but God."

Amunebet changed the subject. "What should I do to prepare for them?"

Joseph knew it would take at least three days for the brothers to get from the border station to the estate. "Instruct the servants to call me by my Egyptian name, Psothom-Phanech. Also, have Asenath and the boys taken to On to visit with their grandparents." He waved broadly at the house and yard. "Make sure the servants clean everything thoroughly."

Amunebet smiled indulgently as he looked at his friend and master. The estate was already clean enough that a person could almost eat from the tiled floors. He saluted smartly and left to instruct the servants. For Joseph the three days passed very slowly. As the time of meeting came closer, he could hardly contain himself. What will my brothers be like? Will they recognize me?

Chapter 15: The Brothers In Egypt

The sons of Jacob entered Egypt in the month of Pakhons. In a normal year, this was the month of planting. Now they had been brought to Joseph's estate.

Joseph, dressed in an ankle-length linen robe, sat stiffly in an armchair on the raised dais in the great hall of his home. A gold collar ringed his neck; gold bands circled his bronzed wrists and biceps. A white headcloth encased in a gold band crowned his head. Amunebet, beside him, leaned on a long staff. On the other side stood Hotpe, the interpreter. Two scribes sat cross-legged on the floor to the left of the dais. White ostrich-feather fans encased in gold shields waved above Joseph, held by servants dressed only in white shentis. Smell of candles and incense permeated the room.

A servant announced, "The Canaanites have arrived."

Joseph tensed. "Let them enter."

Ten men walked through the door. Joseph resisted the urge to shrink at sight of his brothers. He recognized each of them — yet they had changed so much. He could still put a name on each face, though some had grayed and some now had full beards. Simeon, a full head above the other brothers, seemed even bonier than before. Piercing eyes peered out above his large, hooked nose, and totally gray beard. Joseph almost smiled. Simeon must still have the same aggressive personality. Long white scars streaked his face and half of one ear had disappeared. A gold earring dangled from his good ear.

Reuben's huskiness had partially turned to fat. His gray hair, held in place by a leather headband, was wilder than ever on his diminutive head. Joseph could see little change in Judah. His black hair, barely touched with gray at the temples, framed a face still uncompromising and stern, his narrow mouth pursed in a straight line. Levi was a little stooped but his blue eyes remained sharp and observant. Joseph saw few changes in the younger brothers.

Afraid they might recognize him, Joseph rested his elbow on the arm of his chair, holding his hand before his face. He was clean-shaven, as was the Egyptian custom, but he had also been beardless when they had cast him into the pit. He had then been a stripling seventeen-year-old, now filled out at a husky forty plus years, dressed in the finest of Egyptian linen, face and arms tanned as brown as any Egyptian.

Joseph paused for effect, then asked in Egyptian, "How far did you travel?" He listened anxiously for their answers, having difficulty waiting for the interpreter to translate.

“Reuben stepped forward as spokesman. “We traveled through the desert for twenty days, your lordship.”

“Did you have any problems?”

“Only one, your lordship. A dust abubu scattered our donkeys and filled our tents with sand.”

Joseph nodded. “Who are you? What do you want in Egypt?”

“We are herdsmen from Canaan. We’ve come for grain and corn for our families, your lordship.”

Joseph nodded, then leaned back and studied the faces of the brothers, looking into their eyes until they averted them and looked at the floor. Joseph’s eyes slitted. “I feel there is something you are not telling me. You look more like soldiers than herdsmen. Perhaps you came to Egypt to spy on our defenses. You think that because there is famine we will be weak.”

As the translator interpreted what Joseph said, a look of incredulity appeared on their faces. “What?” Judah cried. He looked at Joseph with an expression of mingled fear and surprise.

Joseph looked directly at Judah. “What is your real purpose in coming to Egypt?”

Judah stepped up beside Reuben. “It is as my brother said. We came for corn and grain to feed our families.”

“So, you are brothers?” Joseph cried in a louder voice.

Reuben regained his voice. He gestured at those around him. “We are ten brothers.”

Joseph leaned forward, persisting. “You do not look like brothers. Your father had ten sons?”

Simeon impatiently stepped up by his two older brothers. A dimple appeared in his cheek as he talked. He spoke from the right side of his cruelly twisted mouth. “We are truly twelve brothers.”

Joseph regarded him coldly. “Wait. A few moments ago you said you were ten.”

Simeon’s scar turned scarlet as he frowned.

“Twelve brothers originally,” Reuben interjected quickly, reddening under Joseph’s accusations, “but our youngest brother stayed home with our father, and one is no longer with us.”

“No longer with us?” Joseph paused, a frown on his face. “What does that mean?”

“He is lost.”

Joseph found he enjoyed the discomfiture of the brothers. He pressed his point. “Lost?”

Several brothers hung their heads. Judah spoke, “A wild animal killed him.”

“A wild animal? How did that happen?”

Simeon growled. “We don’t know. We found his bloody coat.”

Joseph smiled faintly between compressed lips and decided to drop that subject. “And your youngest brother?”

“At home, in the tent of our father.”

“He is but a child, then?”

Reuben looked helplessly at his brothers. “No, he is a man.”

“Yet he stays home in the tent of your father? Is he not married?”

Joseph could see the brothers became more uncomfortable by the moment. Judah again answered. “Your Highness, he is married and has six children.” He shrugged helplessly. “But he still dwells with our father.”

Joseph leaned back and smiled. “Oh. Then your father still lives?”

As the interpreter translated the last question, the brothers nodded, almost in unison.

Joseph’s sun-darkened skin could not hide the flush in his cheeks. He paused to control his emotions. “I still think you may be spies. I will test your truth. One will return to your home and bring your youngest brother of whom you speak. Then I will sell you corn and grain.”

The brothers’ faces blanched. Reuben said, “That is impossible!” He turned to his brothers, asking in a low voice, “What do we do now?”

Joseph nodded to Amunebet, who quickly stepped to the door and summoned servants. They hustled the brothers into the now unused brewery and locked the door.

Simeon spat on the dusty floor. “That man appeared genuinely concerned, asking questions about our journey. Then he accuses us of being spies and locks us in here!” He spat again. “He’s two-faced.”

Issachar mused. “I think he tried to make us angry.”

Dan, almost deaf, cupped his hand over his ear and shouted, “What are we going to do?”

Gad stammered, then explained rapidly to Dan, “One of us must return to our father’s tent and bring Benjamin here.”

Dan shouted, “Father will never let him go.”

Reuben nodded. “That is the problem. Which one of us can convince father to let Benjamin come?”

Asher asked, "And what guarantee is there that, if he does come, the Egyptian will release us?"

Zebulon, who had been silent, spoke up. "Judah should go. He is the only one father seems to trust."

One voice after another joined in, suggesting who should go, or arguing about who should not.

Simeon said angrily, "Let's just break down the door and escape." Judah looked at him coldly. "And then what would you do? Walk back to our father empty-handed? My wife and children starve. We must have grain. If it takes bringing Benjamin here to get it, then we bring Benjamin here." Then he added, "Father or no father."

"Let's not be hasty," Reuben said. "We must not hurt father again." Several nodded.

For three days they sat in the brewery, wondering what their fate would be. On the evening of the third day servants ushered them into the great hall again. On purpose Joseph had not brought in the interpreter. Perhaps they would say things they might not say if they knew they were understood.

The brothers had made their decision, but they still argued as they entered. Simeon, angrily looked with baleful eyes at Joseph. "I still think we should just crack their heads and escape."

Reuben looked at him accusingly. "You will never learn! It was you that was so anxious to kill Joseph. How I wish I could have stopped you. I told you not to sin against him, but you did not listen."

Tears came to Joseph's eyes as he listened. He turned quickly away from the arguing brothers huddled together in the center of the great room. When the interpreter entered the room, Reuben said, "We have selected our brother, Judah, to return to our father's tent to bring our youngest brother to you."

Joseph frowned. "I have changed my mind. You shall all go but one who must remain as hostage until the others return." He leaned forward and pointed a ringed finger at Simeon. "You. You alone will remain in prison to await the return of your brothers."

Simeon stepped forward, defiant.

Amunebet clapped his hands. A servant appeared and Amunebet whispered to him. In a few moments the servant returned with a length of rope. While his brothers watched, he bound the fuming Simeon from head to toe. The brothers whispered to him. Joseph heard one say, "Courage brother, We will return quickly so you can be set free."

Reuben said aloud, "We will take care of your families until you return."

Napthali stepped forward. He spoke wistfully through shiny lips, "At least you won't have to face our father when we tell him he must send Benjamin to Egypt."

Simeon just growled. Two servants dragged him from the room.

Joseph said to Amunebet. "Go with them in the morning to the storehouse. Fill their sacks with grain." He then spoke to Reuben, his voice thick. "You will be free to go in the morning. My overseer will arrange for corn to take to your families." He watched as the words were translated.

They filed through the door.

He told Amunebet, "After you fill their sacks and receive their money, place every man's money back in his own sack before you seal it. Also, give them enough provisions for their journey."

Amunebet saluted and hurried out the door. Joseph slumped in his chair, exhausted. He dismissed the servants and sat alone. Tears streaked his tanned cheeks.

The following morning, after loading the donkeys, Amunebet called the brothers together. He counseled them. "No harm will come to your brother unless you fail to return. If you have not returned by six months from this date . . ." He shrugged his shoulders eloquently. "May the gods be with you on your journey."

Anxious to get back to their homes and families, the brothers needed no urging. As they walked, leading their loaded donkeys, they talked over what had happened. Though happy to receive grain so their families would not starve, their happiness was tempered by anticipation of Jacob's reaction to their news.

They were already into the desert when they stopped for noon. As they ate some of the provisions Amunebet had sent with them, Reuben spoke up. "My brothers," he said. "It is normally a twenty-day journey to our home in Hebron, is it not?" The brothers nodded. "If we travel into the night, is it possible we can shorten it to seventeen?"

Again his brothers nodded.

"Our families hunger. We must make every effort to hurry in order to get back to Egypt to save Simeon. I propose we travel into the night."

"Agreed," Judah said. "We have spent enough time away from our families."

They plodded forward through afternoon and evening. Exhausted, they finally stopped at a camp with a well, a few straggly trees, and fire pits where hundreds had camped before them. Several caravans had already bedded down for the night. Wearily the brothers attended camp duties. Reuben took charge. He assigned Levi and Judah to gather dry camel droppings and kindling for a fire. He told Zebulon and Dan to get water; Napthali and Gad to unload the donkeys and put the packs together where they could be easily guarded; and Issachar and Asher to feed and water the animals.

Issachar unloaded his ass and began to feed it from the grain they had purchased. He gave a shout. "My brothers, look here!" They came running. In the dark, starlight glinted off what Issachar held in his hands. "My silver! The full price I paid for my wheat. It's all in the sack."

"Oh, no!" Judah exclaimed. "Now what?"

The brothers ran to where they had placed their own sacks, tearing them open in their haste.

They traveled the remainder of the distance home without event. By traveling each day to the point of exhaustion across the hot waste, they reached their father's tent on the evening of the seventeenth day. They separated, each to his own tent. At first light, they appeared together before Jacob, unrested and anxious.

The aged patriarch, propped up on his cushions, looked from one to the other. "What is it, my sons?" he rumbled. Judah, the spokesman, stood before his father. Though forty-five years of age, he felt as a child before his venerable father. Jacob's eyes pierced him. "Out with it! What happened to your brother, Simeon?"

"We met with the grand vizier, Father," he said. "The man accused us of being spies." He looked around at his brothers helplessly. "He kept Simeon as a hostage and sent us back to bring Benjamin."

"Benjamin!" Jacob exploded. "I will not send Benjamin. Already I have lost Joseph. Now I lose Simeon. Would you have me lose Benjamin, also?" Judah controlled himself. "That is not all, father. On our journey home, when we opened our sacks of corn to feed our donkeys, we discovered our silver had been returned to us." He looked pleadingly at Jacob. "What does it mean?"

Jacob shook his head. "I know not. Who knows the mind of the sly Egyptians? Perhaps they lay a trap for us all." He lay his head back against a tent pole, looking at the top of the tent. "Oh, Joseph. Oh, Simeon." He motioned to Benjamin. "Come my son, sit beside me."

"But what of Simeon?" retorted Reuben impatiently. "Is he to rot in the Egyptian prisons?" In desperation he knelt before his father. "Father, let me take Benjamin. Keep my own two sons as hostages for his life. If I do not return him, then slay them. But let me take Benjamin and I will return him to you unharmed."

The old man looked around at the worried faces. Nodding towards Benjamin, he said solemnly. "His brother is dead and he alone remains with me. If he went with you to Egypt and something happened to him I would go to my grave."

Muttering, Judah stood to leave. He turned to Levi. "I go to look after Simeon's family."

Drought and the scarcity remained sore and oppressive. In three months Jacob's large family had practically exhausted the supply of corn and grain. Jacob called another council. There had been much grumbling as the months rolled by and no provision had been made for Simeon's return. They surrounded Jacob in his tent.

"We have neither seed corn nor grain for baking. Our children cry for bread. What can we do?"

Reuben shrugged. "There is only one thing to do."

Judah added, "We must take Benjamin with us. The Egyptian told us we could not even show our face unless Benjamin was with us. If we do not go soon, Simeon is a dead man and we will all starve."

Jacob lowered his head in his misery. He had wrestled with this problem from the time his sons returned from Egypt. "Why did you even tell them you had a younger brother?"

"Because he asked us!" Reuben exploded. "He accused us of spying and we could not be caught in a lie. He even asked if you, our father, still lived. We answered him the truth. We didn't know he would ask us to bring Benjamin to Egypt."

Judah stood, placing himself directly before his father. "Send Benjamin with us and we can be on our way to get food for our families." He knelt before his father in an attitude of supplication. "If we do not go soon, our children die of starvation. We will all die." He looked around at his brothers. "Father, use me as security. If I don't bring Benjamin back, let the guilt be on me forever."

Napthali said, "Father, if we had gone when we desired, we would have been back already with Simeon and Benjamin and food for our families." "My sons, my sons. I will pray about it tonight. Tomorrow I shall give my answer."

Jacob's red eyes next morning attested to his sleepless night. After the brothers seated themselves in his tent once again, he looked at them, resignation in his expression. "Take Benjamin with you. But take gifts to soften the Egyptian's heart." He reviewed the scarce supplies they still had. "Take oil of balsam, gum of Tragacanth, grape honey, pistachio nuts, and almonds. Alto take double the money so you can pay not only for the new grain but for last time's as well. Take Benjamin and present him to the man in Egypt. I give my consent." He sorrowfully dropped his head to his chest. Tears appeared in his rheumy eyes as he looked up. "I prepare myself to be without any children." He knelt, his head bowed until his forehead rested on the rugs on the floor of the tent. "Oh, Jehovah, please do not take my son from me. Be watchful over him on this journey, I implore you."

Benjamin had never had opportunity to see the world. His thirty-two years had been spent in the shadow of his father's tent. He made his preparations, packed the few things he would need and bid goodbye to his wife, Rahah, and his children.

In light of early dawn, the brothers set forth on their second journey to Egypt. Families watched them go. Jacob stood alone, beholding Benjamin, his dearest possession, leaving on the caravan.

On the same day the ten sons of Israel left Hebron to return to Egypt, Joseph began a tour through the nomes of Egypt. He needed to check on the smooth distribution of grain from the storehouses. For his journey he used one of Pharaoh's small mensh, not much larger than a small rowboat. The river was too shallow for his bark. The mensh carried ten sweep oars and a square, horizontally rigged sail. Even if the northerly winds did not blow, with strong oarsmen Joseph would be able to complete his inspection tour. He spent most of his time on the rudder platform. He never tired of viewing the majesty of creation which surrounded him. They passed several fields where men in loincloths toiled up the river bank, leather bottles filled with water to irrigate their meager clumps of corn.

As they sailed up the river, he could hear background shouts of the lookout on the bow. "The depth of a reed and four cubits; the depth of a reed and five cubits." The oarsmen sat silently, letting the southward-blowing breeze carry them against the current. The sailor on the sweep pulled back and forth, keeping the ship in the center of the channel. Often the boat scraped bottom and the oarsmen had to lift it off the sandbars.

Joseph's thoughts kept returning to his brothers. It has been almost six months since they appeared before me. No word has come from them. Simeon is still locked up. Are my brothers ignoring my threat? Did they see through my disguise? Was I wrong in deceiving them concerning my identity? He recalled a proverb that Amunebet had told him many years before: "He who sails with falsehood for a cargo does not reach land." Egyptians believed in truth and honor. They called their principle of truth, maat. *Was I less than truthful with my brothers? I did not really intend to deceive them — my only desire was to gain information and discover their feelings. Perhaps I should have told them who I was.*

With his mind so filled with questions and concerns, Memphis was before them before he realized it. He looked up and saw the wharf high above the water. A mass of fishermen lined dry banks attempting to catch a meal from the shallow stream. Dockhands stood on the wharf, curiously watching the approaching ship.

Joseph stepped onto the rickety ladder which led up to the wharf. He had notified the vizier, by land courier, of his coming. City officials greeted him. They rode through the city to inspect storage facilities and to observe the long lines of those waiting for grain. Bearers carried Joseph through the once thriving manufacturing district of the city, a vast spread of mud-brick buildings which had housed potters, goldsmiths, embalmers and coffin-makers. Now many shops lay idle. Little money existed to pay for any services. Joseph and his guide continued westward through the city to the home of Snefru, the nobleman who had invited Joseph to be his guest for the evening. Snefru tried to interest Joseph in a game of senet, but after a few moves Joseph lost interest. He had a restless spirit. Finally, he asked to borrow Snefru's team and chariot.

He changed into a simple shenti. Through the dusty, rutted streets, then far westward into the Libyan hills he rode as he wrestled with answer to his concerns. This land was a glaring hell of harsh, red sand and stone. When Joseph started his return it was dark. From a high vantage point he looked down over the dark Nile valley where Egypt slept. Stopping his fiery team, he stepped from the chariot. He knelt, holding tightly to the reins. Creaking of leather harness and horse's shuffling hoofs were the only sounds; the nervous pull of the reins in his hands, the only movement. He prayed, "Jehovah, I have faith that through Thee all things will work for the best good of my people. Calm my mind with the knowledge of my brothers' return." He prayed on into the night, praising God for bounteous blessings, asking for strength to overcome obstacles and difficulties. His heart at peace, he stepped back into the chariot.

Nervously, the horses strained at their bits, anxious to be off. They fought for their heads as Joseph loosened the reins then plunged down the slope, the chariot rumbling over ruts and stones.

A fortnight passed before Joseph returned to his estate. The work of scribes and overseers in distributing grain from warehouses and granaries pleased him. Everything worked as he had envisioned. The Pharaoh's coffers filled with gold. Pharaoh and Joseph had gained the hearts of the people. Everyone had sufficient grain to eat.

Coming home was the best part of being away. Joseph strode up the path towards his estate. Manasseh and Ephraim tried to outdo each other to get to him first. He picked them up and held them high in his arms, showering kisses on each young face. Asenath greeted him warmly. He set the boys down and held her close, his head buried in her fragrant hair. He loved being loved.

After a pleasant dinner with his family he went to his office. Papyrus reports from border forts overflowed his desk. It took him some time to get through the lists. He had almost given up when he saw the names: Judah, Reuben, Levi ... He skimmed to the bottom. Benjamin! They came again!

Chapter 16: The Brothers Return

Joseph instructed Amunebet: "When my brothers come, bring them once more to my house."

"It shall be as you command."

"I will have lunch with them. Invite some city officials from On.;

We will make it a grand affair."

"Egyptian customs prohibit sitting to eat with foreigners."

Joseph smiled. "Then why have they been eating with me all these years? Everyone knows I am not a child of the Nile." He sat in contemplation. "And Amunebet, one more thing. When my brothers come, seat them according to age — Reuben first and on around until Benjamin is seated at my right." He smiled at his own subtlety. "It will cause them to wonder."

The brothers, dusty and tired from their twenty-day journey from Hebron, followed their Egyptian guide through the gate of the estate. Amunebet greeted them on the step of the main house. Then he called for slaves to take their animals to the stables.

"Welcome back to Egypt and to the house of my master," he said. "May the blessings of the god of the Nile be upon you."

Judah bowed. "Thank you kind sir. There is something, however, we must tell you. When we departed from your land with the corn and provisions you so graciously gave us, by some mistake, the silver with which we purchased the corn was placed back in our sacks." He and his brothers looked with dread at Joseph's steward. Judah continued. "We found it as we journeyed home. We brought silver to replace that which was returned by mistake. We also brought silver to purchase more corn."

Amunebet shrugged. "I know not of the silver you talk about," he replied glibly. "What is past is past." Inwardly he smiled as he noticed the obvious relief on the brothers' faces. After making them comfortable in the guest quarters, he left them, returning a few minutes later with a relieved Simeon — dressed in a fine robe of Egyptian linen. Amunebet left, but stood outside the door, listening.

They all talked at once. The brothers seemed genuinely interested in Simeon. They greeted him and asked about his time in Egypt. They did not have long to visit. Slaves brought bowls in which the brothers washed their faces, arms and feet. Other slaves brought fresh linen robes to wear. When washed and clothed, Amunebet himself came to their quarters to lead them to the luncheon. He seated them in comfortable chairs around the large table, each according to age. The brothers looked at each other, eyes large with wonder. Was this some kind of magic — that they should be seated in just the order in which they sat in their father's tent?

Servants, naked to the waist, stood around the room, waiting to serve the guests. In one corner two musicians played harp and flute. The harpist sang softly to the accompaniment of the instruments. Light streamed through windows high above their heads, casting dusty sunbeams on the table. At the head of the table, the master's chair remained empty.

Joseph swept into the room, dressed in a fine, purple-striped robe. A purple headscarf adorned his head, held in place by a gold band. A beaded collar girdled his neck. Below it a huge gold amulet, held by a gold chain, draped over his chest. Next to the amulet dangled a wrinkled leather pouch. His eyes sparkled as he saw the brothers, who immediately scraped their chairs back and knelt in obeisance to him. The dream he had as a youth flowed before his eyes. He smiled.

Rising to their feet, Judah and Reuben stepped forward and bowed low before Joseph's chair. "Our father sent you presents." They set the boxes and ornamental caskets before Joseph. Still bowing, they retreated to their seats.

"When you return to your father's tent, please give him my thanks." Joseph looked at the group. "Speaking of your father, is he well and yet alive?"

Judah, eyes on the floor, answered, "Your servant, our father, is alive and in good health."

Joseph's eyes shifted from Judah and Reuben to Benjamin. "Is this your younger brother of whom you spoke?"

They nodded.

Joseph looked at his full brother. He had not seen him for so many years. He ached to step to him and embrace him. Benjamin was tall and fair. He had sharp features, a high forehead, a full, generous mouth. His eyes were a deep, clear blue, unclouded, giving a feeling of trust. Benjamin smiled at Joseph. His eyes crinkled.

Dignitaries arrived from On. Amunebet seated them at a separate table so they could maintain their dietary laws. Joseph sat at the table with his brothers, with Benjamin on his immediate right. He nodded to Amunebet.

Immediately, aproned servants scurried into the room. Several carried large pitchers. They moved from place to place, pouring wine into beakers. The pitchers had been hanging deep in the well for several days, and the wine was cool and refreshing. Others carried main dishes from the buffet. There was veal, mutton, fish, duck, and goose. Joseph smiled at the obvious surprise of his brothers at seeing such food. He remembered that in Canaan, even in times of plenty, meat was considered a delicacy, served no more than twice a month.

Meat, game, fruit, bread and pastries filled the long table. Servants made sure no one went thirsty, refilling goblets with beer or wine. Joseph, as master, was served first and with larger portions than any other. Many times during the meal he leaned over to put a choice piece of meat or bread, or a quince jelly, on Benjamin's plate. Benjamin looked embarrassed to receive so much attention. He looked around the table with a helpless expression. Eating all that was before him would be an impossible task.

The atmosphere at the banquet relaxed. People chatted gaily with each other. Joseph could feel Benjamin's frustration; his stares and frowns as he obviously tried to remember. Joseph smiled, his eyes dancing. He would keep up the charade yet a little longer. Eager to find out more about his younger brother, he asked about Benjamin's home, his wife, his children. The banquet lasted far into the afternoon. Even after all had reached a point of satiety, Joseph had servants bring more desserts. It was a king's feast. Soon the heads of several of the Egyptians nodded. None of the brothers dozed. Others still looked puzzled, as if they did not understand what was happening. Joseph knew they had observed how he had spent most of his time talking with Benjamin, and sharing his plate with the youngest brother.

When the bounteous meal was over, Judah stepped forward once again. "Most noble one," he began. "Our father asked me to personally deliver this letter to you." He handed Joseph a rolled parchment.

Joseph snapped the seal and unrolled it. He read: "From thy servant, Jacob, son of Isaac, grandson of Abraham the Hebrew, the prince of God, to the powerful and wise king, the revealer of secrets, king of Egypt, greeting.

"Be it known to my lord, the famine has been sore upon us in the land of Canaan, and I sent my sons to thee to buy us a little food for our support. I do not see with my eyes, as they have become very heavy through age, as well as with daily weeping for my son, Joseph, who was lost before me."

Joseph's eyes filled with tears. He turned quickly away from his brothers, and hurriedly left the room. In the anteroom, his head against the wall, tears flowed freely. Pulling himself together, he read the rest of the letter. "I commanded them to go to Egypt, and you considered them as spies in the land. Have we not heard concerning you that you did interpret Pharaoh's dream and did speak truly unto him?: How then did you not know in your wisdom whether my sons are spies are not?"

Joseph chuckled at his father's logic. He could almost see his father's wrath as he made that statement. He reread that part, then continued. "My beloved son, Benjamin, comes to you with my sons. Take heed of him. He is close to my heart. Send them all back in peace."

Joseph slowly rolled the parchment. He held it to his breast for a moment. It was the first word between his father and himself in twenty-three years. He composed himself and returned to the banquet room. He smiled and dropped the parchment on the table. "Men of Canaan," he said, "in this letter your father informed me of your intentions. All now seems well with your story. Tonight you may fill your sacks with corn and in the morning be on your way home." As the interpreter translated what he had said, he turned and stared at Benjamin.

Benjamin returned the stare, his head cocked, a flicker of recognition in his eyes. Joseph smiled wistfully and turned away.

Judah bowed. "We are indebted to you for the bounteous meal and for your hospitality. We will report your kindness to our father."

"Now, Lord, with your permission," Levi said, " we must load while there is still light. We need to get an early start in the morning."

Joseph nodded. He waved his hand in a signal of dismissal and leaned back in his chair as they filed out. Joseph and Amunebet remained alone in the great hall. He sighed. "What do you think?"

"The youngest son seems to recognize you."

"I dropped a few hints. It is good for him to wonder." Joseph sighed. "The drama draws to a close." Idly, he ran his index finger around the rim of his silver bowl. "I wanted one more test before I revealed myself to my brothers. Now I wonder if I shouldn't just tell them."

Amunebet cleared his throat, but said nothing.

Joseph looked curiously at him. "If you have something to say, say it."

"My Lord, you have told me many times that your slavery and time in prison was a test to you. That your god wanted to find what you were made of — whether you were strong enough to pass the test." He shrugged eloquently. "You said strength only comes after a trial of your faith. If that is true, then is it not fair to test your brothers? Should they not prove themselves before you open your heart to them?"

Joseph sighed. "You are right, Amunebet. Just as a tree without a deep root system will blow over in the first wind, so we need to have the deep kind of roots that only come by trial. There is one more test. I must find out if they protect Benjamin, or if they are willing to sacrifice him as they did me." He looked at Amunebet. "Fill the men's sacks with grain, and put every man's money in his sack's mouth. Then put my silver cup . . ." he handed it to Amunebet ". . . in the sack of the youngest."

Smiling, Amunebet bowed low and left. Joseph, on the throne chair, sighed. The game had exhausted him. Oh, he thought. If I could only trust my brothers I would not have to go through this charade. I could have revealed myself to them the first time I saw them. But this has to be. Are they of the same character as when they sold me to the Midianites? Or have they changed? That is the question that must be answered. With donkeys loaded heavily with corn, Reuben and his brothers passed through the gates of Joseph's estate. The burning orb of the sun rose above the eastern desert. Each brother carried a filled water skin. They joked and sang as they took the trail to the Bitter Lakes. They had done what Jacob had sent them to do. They had plentiful corn for their families. Benjamin was safe. And their brother, Simeon, was again with them. Napthali sang an old shepherd song as he walked. The brothers joined in as they made their way further into the desert.

Something troubled Benjamin. He had not slept well the night before. He kept seeing the vizier's face, kept hearing the vizier's voce. What was it? Was he dreaming? Had he heard that voice before? Could it be. . .? No, he tried to put the thought from his mind. But as he walked, the same nagging thought surfaced, again and again.

After six hours, men and animals were tired. At a spot where they could rest, Reuben called a halt. "We will rest here until it is cooler." The men set their packs down. Before they could take the sacks from sweating donkeys they heard a noise from the direction from which they had come.

Joseph waited an hour after his brothers left before calling Amunebet. The steward noted how tired his master looked. "Are you all right, my lord?" he asked.

Joseph smiled wanly. "I am fine. It will be good to have this business over with."

Amunebet nodded in understanding. "Sometimes it seems difficult to do those things which have to be done."

Reflecting on Amunebet's statement, Joseph mused, "God has purposes in our lives. For some reason, He has purpose for my brothers. I trust God has made ample provision beforehand to achieve His purposes, including his purposes in our lives." He sighed. "My friend," Joseph said, "harness a chariot and go after my brothers. Take one bowman. When you catch up with them, say, 'Why have you rewarded good with evil?' They will be surprised by your question. Then ask, 'Which one of you has taken my master's silver cup?' After their denials, search each sack, beginning with the oldest on down to the youngest."

"What happens when I find it?"

"Watch their reactions. See whether they defend my younger brother, or whether they condemn him. Then bring them back to stand before me." Amunebet saluted, spun on his heel, and was gone. Minutes later Joseph heard the clatter of the chariot's wheels on the stone courtyard. Then all was still.

* * *

The brothers watched as the chariot, pulled by two white horses frothing at their bits, drew up to them. Two men stood in the chariot. Issachar recognized Amunebet first. "It is the steward of the grand vizier," he cried.

Simeon sprang forward. "Now what does he want?" he growled. Reuben faced him. "Whatever it is, you keep out of it. We do not need your temper."

Amunebet wheeled the chariot sharply, throwing up a cloud of sand and dust. He jumped down and stalked to the tight circle of men. A frown darkened his face; his brows knitted tightly together.

"So, I finally overtook you. I rushed after you this morning at my master's command." He waited for his words to sink in, giving them a dramatic effect. He asked the question he had rehearsed on the way. "Why is it you repay evil for good? Did not my master treat you well and give you every consideration?"

Reuben, a puzzled look on his florid face, looked at the brothers. They looked equally puzzled. He turned to the steward. "What is it you say? Evil for good?"

"Need you ask?" Amunebet said. "I speak of my master's silver drinking cup. It has been stolen and only you were in the room."

Simeon jumped forward, reaching for his sword. Reuben held him back. "Why should we do such a thing? We have plenty of money. We have been honest with you. Not only did we bring our younger brother with us from the land of Canaan, as your master requested, but we even brought back the money for last year's grain and offered it to you. Why, then, should we steal anything?"

Pushing his way through the brothers, Judah advanced on the steward. "We are innocent men. If you find the cup in the possession of any one of us, then let that person die, and the rest of us will be your slaves." A murmur of approval came from the brothers. Simeon, still red of face, also nodded.

"Yes, search us!" shouted Reuben.

Calmly, Amunebet looked around at the brothers. "No one will die. However, if we find the master's silver cup in the possession of any one of you, that person shall be my servant. The rest of you can continue on your journey. Unload your sacks."

The brothers sprang to the task, quickly pulling the full sacks from the backs of the small donkeys. Amunebet noted the position of each man's sack, oldest to youngest. Nodding to the bowman who kept his eye on the group, he moved to the first sack. After opening it, he sifted down through the corn with his hands. Reuben, looking over his shoulder, for his was the first bag, shuddered. Bad luck again! The silver payment for the grain was again there. But Amunebet found no silver cup. He moved to the next sack, and the next, searching each sack thoroughly. Each of the brothers in turn breathed a sigh of relief when he finished their sack: Reuben, Simeon, Levi, Judah, Issachar, Zebulon, Dan, Napthali, Gad, and Asher.

Amunebet came to the sack of Benjamin. He wiped the streaming sweat from his face, adjusted his sword belt, then bent to his task. As he ran his hand into the corn, it struck something hard — something he knew would be there for he had placed it there himself. He slowly pulled out the silver cup and held it at arms length above his head. "Now what say you?" he asked the now silent group.

They turned as one, looking at Benjamin. Reuben was first to speak. "Why, Benjamin, why?" He reached down and grabbed the hem of his garment, symbolically tearing it. Each of the others did likewise.

Benjamin stood by his donkey, a lonely and accused man. Soberly he said, "I have no idea how it got there."

Levi stalked to him. "We are shamed by you."

Dan started to his youngest brother's defense, but stopped at a nod from Reuben.

Without being told by Amunebet, Reuben commanded. "Let us load the grain and corn and return once more to Egypt."

The brothers moodily complied. With Amunebet leading the way in Joseph's chariot, they started their sad journey back.

Chapter 17: "I Am Joseph"

Joseph had never felt so impatient. He paced back and forth, feeling that on this one test depended his future relationships with his brothers. He walked to the women's quarters. Asenath sat on the floor playing with Ephraim. He had a crocodile toy he pulled with a string. As it moved, its jaw opened and closed. Each time the jaw opened, his mother made a frightened face, and Ephraim laughed gaily. Joseph rejoiced at the happy family sight. Not wanting to disturb them with his worries, he just greeted them, then sat watching.

Asenath, perceptive as always of Joseph's moods, noticed his frown. As soon as Ephraim's little game finished, she shooed him outside to play. She motioned for Joseph to sit beside her. Silently waiting, she ran her fingers through his hair, dragging them softly down his cheeks. After a long silence, when it was obvious that Joseph was not going to tell her what troubled him, she breathed, "My husband. My dear lord. What troubles you?"

"Is it so obvious?"

She smiled indulgently.

Joseph sighed, then explained the test he had given his brothers. When he described putting the silver cup in Benjamin's sack, she looked at him wide-eyed. Her discomfiture then dissolved before a rush of inner laughter. She clapped her hands in delight.

Frustrated, Joseph lifted his shoulders, then let them sag. "I desire very much to see if they will now be united as brothers, or whether they still bear resentment to Benjamin as they did to me." He pushed her away so he could look into her eyes. "Do you think they will send Benjamin back alone with Amunebet, or will they come as brothers should? United?"

Asenath did not answer immediately, but pulled him back and continued to stroke his hair. Finally she whispered, "My dear one. I do not know your brothers as well as you. But I do feel they are now mature men and will not let you divide them." She smiled again. "I think your test is delightful." Seeing that she still had not penetrated his moroseness, she asked, "Shall we play a game to divert your attention?"

Usually, Joseph loved to play senet with his wife, but surely not now! As usual, Asenath had her way. She clapped her hands and ordered the servant to set up the game. He brought in the square playing board, with its squares called oyoon, or eyes. Joseph and Asenath each placed twelve kelbs on the playing board. Before, Joseph had always played aggressively, trying to capture Asenath's kelb by coming up along side and trapping it with his kelb on each side. The game required much concentration, and this day Joseph had none. Asenath beat him repeatedly, laughing gaily each time she took one of his kelb from the board.

Frustrated, Joseph put down his playing piece. "When they come," he said, "and if they pass the test, I will introduce myself to my brothers. I will want to present my family. Please be ready, and have the boys dressed in their finest linen." He excused himself and returned to his office. There he pored over endless papyrus. Today none of them captured his attention. The sun descended low in the heavens as he listened for Amunebet's return. At last he heard the confusion of sounds signaling their arrival.

Amunebet entered the office brusquely. As soon as he stepped inside a broad smile appeared on his face. He handed Joseph the silver cup. Joseph could see he really enjoyed this little game. "They wait your judgment in the great hall, Master."

"All of them?" Joseph asked.

"All of them."

"Anything you would report?"

"I think you will see for yourself, Master."

Joseph smiled for the first time. He pushed through the door and strode deliberately to the dais where his chair waited. He sat down, cupping his chin in his hand. The cup dangled from his other hand. Several servants moved onto the dais and started waving ostrich fans gently above his head, cooling him. His scribes and interpreter sat before him, ready.

A slanting sunray filled with dancing dust shone from the upper window. It fell on the brothers who had cast themselves face down on the floor.

Amunebet and his bowman stood on either side, giving a show of guarding the brothers. A host of cooks, servants, slaves and yardmen crowded outside the door, wondering what had happened.

"Well, Canaanites, sons of the father, Jacob, whom you have told me about, and brothers all," Joseph said, "I did not expect to see you again so soon. Stand up." As they stood before him, he continued, looking at each who would look him in the eye. "How could you repay my good with evil?" The brothers hung their heads and looked away, except for Simeon who stared at Benjamin with a look of disgust.

Joseph asked, "Who is the guilty one? Or are all of you guilty?"

Judah stepped forward. "We are all guilty before you, my lord. How the cup came to be in the sack of Benjamin we do not know. Nevertheless, we shall all be your slaves."

"That will not be so," said Joseph. "Only he in whose sack the cup was found will be my servant. The rest of you leave in peace and take provisions to your father and your families." He smiled kindly. "We would not want to leave your father childless and without food to eat."

A heavy silence filled the room. The brothers looked at Judah, who bowed low before Joseph. "Let me make it clear, my lord. The youngest will not be separated from us. None of us can return to the tent of our father without Benjamin. Our father, an old man, has already lost one son of his favorite wife. If we returned without Benjamin he would surely die of a broken heart. I pledged myself as surety. Therefore, my lord, I pray thee, let me stay in place of Benjamin. I will be a servant to you so Benjamin can go home to his father. It cannot be otherwise."

Judah's impassioned plea moved Joseph, but he wanted one more proof. "No. The law is plain. Take this cup and go from me. Leave your brother as a slave. Judgment for a thief is to be a slave."

Judah spoke with indignation. "A cup for the life of my brother! You could give us a thousand silver cups and it would make no difference. We will not leave our brother for all the silver in Egypt." He stepped back, hands on hips. "If necessary, we will die rather than leave him." Leaning toward his brothers, Joseph asked, "Then why did you forsake your brother, Joseph, and sell him for twenty pieces of silver?"

The brothers looked at each other in astonishment. How could...? Then a look of understanding came into their faces. But of course. He was a diviner! Only Benjamin looked confused. Then, as he saw the guilt written on the faces of his brothers, a look of shock replaced the confusion on his face.

Reuben stepped forward beside Judah. "We have lived these many years with a cloud of sin over our heads. It is important that we clear it up at this time." The other brothers murmured amongst themselves. Reuben held up a hand for silence. "I, Reuben, break the vow I took almost twenty-five years ago. Let it be known to all men that a beast did not kill our brother, Joseph, but we, his brothers, sold him into slavery. Let it be known and dealt with. But as for our youngest brother, Benjamin, nothing must happen to him. I will bear the blame for what happened before. Let me stand now in Benjamin's stead. I am the oldest. It is my responsibility."

The brothers, pale and wan, waited in dread for the vizier's reaction. Joseph stood, the last rays of sunlight on his face. In the light, tears glistened in his eyes like jewels. "It is enough," he said huskily. "Amunebet, please clear the hall of all Egyptians. I would be alone with these men."

Amunebet, tears glistening in his own eyes, urged the scribes and servants out of the room. As he left, he closed the door gently behind him. Joseph, heedless of the tears on his face, stretched out his arms to his brothers. "Men of Canaan," he cried, "I am your brother, Joseph."

A shocked silence.

Benjamin shouted, "I knew it. I knew it." He stumbled forward and up the steps, throwing his arms around the brother who had been lost.

The others stood in confusion.

"Joseph. Joseph," Benjamin cried as they embraced. "You are you. Of course it is you. I felt it when I sat beside you last night."

"My brother, Benjamin," Joseph said through tears. Instinctively his hand went to the small sack hanging from his neck. He pulled it, snapping the string, then opened it. There was a small round, green stone, worn smooth by the fondling of twenty-three years.

Benjamin clasped Joseph's hands, tears flowing into his graying beard. Joseph, still holding Benjamin, turned to his brothers. They stood looking uncertain, unsure of what to do. A twinkle in his eye, Joseph spoke. "It is good that we are twelve brothers once again."

He put his arm around Benjamin's shoulders. Together they stepped from the dais to join the brothers. Many still stared, unable to comprehend. All had paled at Reuben's confession. Now, many blushed as they thought of what had happened.

Simeon spoke first. Angrily he asked, "Why did you trick us?"

"I had to test you," Joseph answered. "I needed to prove to myself that you had changed — that you were no longer the brothers I knew." He smiled. "I want you to know that I, too, have changed. I am no longer the selfish and spoiled brother you threw into the pit."

Reuben blustered. "But what of...?"

Joseph raised a hand to silence him. "Let the past be forgotten. Be not grieved nor angry with yourselves that you sold me as a slave bound for Egypt. God wanted me here so I could be an instrument in His hands in preserving the lives of our people." He looked around at the brothers, noting tears in some eyes. "Stay with me for a few days. Then you can load your animals and go together back to our father's tent. Tell him that Joseph is not dead, but lives, and desires to speak to him. Tell him that I plead with him to come to Egypt where I can look out for all of you. You shall settle here in rich pasture."

An audible sigh of relief came from the brothers.

Joseph smiled to himself. "Amunebet," he called.

Amunebet stepped smartly into the room. "Sir?"

"Bring Asenath and my sons. I would have my brothers meet my family." As Amunebet stepped back out, Joseph said to his brothers. "We shall eat and drink and be merry, all twelve of us together." He turned to Judah. "When you tell Father, be gentle with him. His heart has been sorely bruised."

Asenath, followed by Manasseh and Ephraim, entered the room. An immediate hush settled over the brothers. Asenath had never looked so beautiful. She had pulled her hair back in a tight bow and wore a light blue linen robe.

Joseph stepped quickly to her. "My brothers," he said. "May I introduce to you my wife, Asenath." He reached down and picked up his sons, one in each arm. "These are my sons, Manasseh and Ephraim."

For the first time since returning to Joseph's house, the brothers broke into large smiles. They stepped forward, all talking at once as they introduced themselves to Joseph's family. Joseph watched, his heart full. He motioned again to Amunebet. "Have a scribe write a letter to Pharaoh telling him about my brothers. Tell him we are one once again. He will understand. We have talked many times about my family and what would happen if we were reunited. Send the letter by special messenger." Amunebet bowed and hurried out.

The brothers stayed with Joseph for a full week. More than twenty years had passed since Jacob had believed Joseph dead. A day or so more now did not seem to matter. The brothers spent time with Joseph, with Asenath and the boys. Joseph treated them royally, giving feasts every evening in their honor.

A letter came from Pharaoh. Joseph read it to his brothers. "I am pleased," he read, "that you are reunited with your family. I give my gracious consent that all of your family should come to Egypt. You may allot them room to settle according to your best judgment." The letter went on to give permission for Joseph to give his brothers donkeys to carry goods back to Canaan, and also wagons to be used to bring their families back to Egypt. Pharaoh ended his letter with an admonition to the brothers. "Pick up your little ones and your wives and your father and come. Look not to your household goods for you shall be provided in this land with all you need. When you come into your land, take your father and his people and his whole house and bring them down to me."

The week passed quickly, but the brothers anxiously looked forward to return to their families in Hebron. As they loaded their belongings and the corn Joseph had given them on their pack animals, Joseph, with several servants trailing, stepped from the house. He called Reuben, hugged him, kissed him on both cheeks, then presented him with a complete change of clothing — a beautiful and colorful linen robe. Each brother came up in turn, receiving Joseph's love tokens. Finally Benjamin stepped up. As he embraced his younger brother, tears ran in little rivulets down Joseph's tanned cheeks. He handed Benjamin a leather bag filled with coins. Then, before Benjamin could protest, Joseph waved his bejeweled hand to a servant. The servant stepped forward, his arms draped with beautiful brocaded and finely woven expensive clothing. Joseph picked up one after another of the fine robes, hanging them on the protesting Benjamin's arms.

After their last goodbye, the brothers went through the gate of Joseph's estate. Another surprise awaited them on the road to Hebron. An entire caravan met them: ten oxen-pulled wagons loaded with supplies for the journey; thirty two-wheeled carts pulled by mules; ten asses loaded with luxurious gifts for Jacob from the land of Egypt; ten other she-asses loaded with grain, wine, preserves, smoked meats, and other foodstuffs. A driver sat on the buckseat of each wagon. The assemblage was as large as any caravan the brothers had ever seen pass their oasis at Mamre. It was truly a magnificent sight.

Chapter 18: Israel Comes to Egypt

Lustily, the brothers chanted glad songs of home. But the songs did not completely conceal their worry. How would they tell their father that his favorite son, whom he had given up for dead, lived? And, should they tell him the truth now about how they sold Joseph into slavery so many years before? They feared Jacob might actually die from the news. So, as they traveled, the brothers discussed how Jacob should be told — and how much he should be told. Judah stubbornly insisted it was time for truth. "For," he said, "hasn't father suspected us all these years?"

Because of the wagons and the caravan's size, the brothers did not dare challenge the sandy desert waste. They chose, instead, to travel the Way of the Philistines trail which led up the coast of the great sea. After passing the frontier fortress, they turned left through the wilderness of Gaza. Traveling mostly at night, they made their way through the land of the Philistines, passing near Gaza, the Philistine seaport. The final phase of the journey was the short inland march from the great sea through the hills to Hebron, the slowest stretch of the entire journey. The caravan bounced through rough and stony hills. As they approached Mamre, the cloud of dust cast into the air by the caravan attracted the attention of everyone in sight.

Rahah, Benjamin's wife, ran to Jacob's tent. "Father," she cried. "A huge caravan appears to be coming here." She pulled back the flap, then recognizing the brothers walking in the lead of the animals, exclaimed, "It is Reuben, and Simeon, and Judah! Your sons are back from Egypt. They come with men and carts and many more asses than they set out with." Even as she spoke, the brothers arrived. They pushed Benjamin forward, anxious that Jacob see him. Rahah rushed to her husband. They walked arm in arm to Jacob's tent. "Peace and good health," Benjamin called.

Reuben entered Jacob's tent, throwing the flap back so all was exposed to view. He put his arm on Jacob's shoulder, guiding his father's hand to rest on Benjamin's arm. "Here is Benjamin, safely returned to your tent. Here also is Simeon." He gestured towards the caravan. "We bring also an abundance of food and rich presents from the grand vizier of Egypt."

With Reuben's arm for support, Jacob laboriously struggled to his feet. Shading his eyes from the sun's glare, he walked outside. Somewhat bewildered, he looked over the vast caravan of goods. "My sons," he said, a tremor in his voice, "praise the Lord that you are home once again."

Tears streaked his cheeks as he embraced Simeon. He had never expected to see this son again. He embraced Benjamin again, and left his hand fondly on Benjamin's arm as he embraced his sons in turn.

Benjamin helped Jacob back into the tent. The brothers clustered around. "Father," Benjamin began as soon as Jacob was seated. "You were concerned about the grand vizier of Egypt, and why he asked that I travel there. We were all puzzled as to why he kept asking about you and your health. Is that not so?"

Jacob shrugged his agreement.

Benjamin sat next to his father and took both his father's hands in his. "Father, once again he asked about you. He showed great concern for your health and your welfare."

His white beard quivered on his chest as again Jacob nodded.

Benjamin's eyes brimmed. "Father, the grand vizier of Egypt is concerned about you because he is your long-lost son, Joseph."

Jacob did not seem to comprehend. He tilted his head, looking quizzically at his youngest son.

"Father, he is Joseph. The vizier and Joseph are one. He is your son and our brother."

Jacob finally found his tongue. "But how... How could that be? His coat was brought to me, bloodied and torn. He was dead..."

"No, father. He never was dead." Wanting to spare his brothers some pain, Benjamin continued. "He was sold as a slave to Egypt. There, with the Lord's help, he has flourished and now is second only to Pharaoh."

Jacob shook his head in disbelief. "Would you have evidence of this miracle?"

Reuben motioned with his arm. "Look at our train. Joseph himself sent twenty asses for you, loaded with the riches of Egypt."

Judah chimed in. "Yes, and the wagons sent by Pharaoh shall carry us all down to see your son. It is his plan that you should come. He has allocated us fat pastures where we can live and prosper. The land will be a settling place for our people."

Jacob closed his eyes. His lips moved silently. Then opening his eyes, he raised them to the heavens. "Blessed be the name of the Lord!" His face looked serene and his eyes had a distant look in them. "I will go down. I will see Joseph before I die."

Jacob stewed night and day about the decision to go to Egypt. How could he leave the hills he loved, the graves of his loved ones, to go to a strange land? But his son beckoned and Jacob's heart was torn. He wanted to see Joseph, but he was not anxious to transport the entire tribe — bag and baggage — to the land of the dead. His sons prevailed. Finally they were packed. It had been difficult to decide what to take. Mamre had been Jacob's home for almost thirty-five years. They loaded what they could and sold or gave away what they could not.

As they started, Jacob thought of the beginning of his journey from Haran so long before. He thought of Abraham and his wanderings. During a famine, Abraham, too, had gone to Egypt to dwell as a stranger. The thought of Abraham brought needed comfort to him. His joy was keen at the prospect of seeing Joseph, but he experienced much sadness at having to leave his beloved Mamre. To go to Egypt, the land of tombs, was bad enough. But the tombs he left behind brought his sharpest pain: Rachel's wayside grave; Machpelah, the double cave Abraham had bought as a burial place. There lay the bodies of Abraham, Sarah, Isaac, Rebecca, and Leah.

Late summer came before Israel wound up his affairs and the ponderous train left the grove of Mamre by Hebron. The caravan of the migrating tribe crept noisily — like a highly-colored caterpillar — forward; slow moving, enveloped by clouds of dust raised by hoofs of trotting flocks, donkeys, and heavy wagons. People of Beersheba had watched many caravans pass through on their way to or from Egypt, but never had they seen such a gaily decorated tribe as this. They gawked at the bearded men in heavy desert cloaks and felt-ringed head cloths. Women, hair in braids on their shoulders, silver and bronze bracelets on their wrists, rode in two-wheeled Egyptian wagons. Silver coins shone on their foreheads. Henna reddened their nails. Infants lay swaddled in great, soft wrappings with brocaded borders.

Teams of mules gaily decorated with glass beads, driven by Egyptian servants, pulled carriages and carts filled with people, and baggage wagons loaded with household goods, leather water bottles, and forage. People of Beersheba looked with awe on the special litter Joseph provided for Jacob. Never had they seen such a vehicle: one of Pharaoh's own palanquins. The litter had a woven reed back rest and sides adorned with hieroglyphics. Rich purple-velvet curtains hung at the windows. Bronze carrying poles undergirded the chair. The brothers had carefully tucked Jacob into the gilded carrying chair, then strapped the chair on the backs of two asses. Jacob would ride to Egypt in style befitting a prince

— for a prince he was: Jacob, the patriarch. Israel; God's chosen servant.

Beersheba had been their first travel goal. "We stop here," he called. "Here," he told his sons, "my father, Isaac, was born. Here, Rebecca readied him for his journey to Haran. Here grows the sacred tree under which Abraham worshipped. Here I will celebrate one last time. Here I will ask the One God for direction and counsel."

Jacob had set forth with flocks and possessions; with sons and sons' sons; with daughters and daughters' sons. Mentally he counted. Seventy sons, grandsons, and great-grandsons along with wives, daughters, drivers and servants — a huge conclave of people. Jacob felt a savage pride as he contemplated this people — a people he had been promised would become a mighty nation. He stood at Beersheba, dressed in a long, dark red robe. The fine wool of his kofia was fringed unevenly across his forehead. It lay in folds about his neck and shoulders and fell softly on his robe, open at the front to reveal his embroidered under-garment.

He thought of the sacred tree of Abraham. The giant tamarisk stood on a slight hill in the village center, planted by Abraham himself, who also built a stone altar at its base. The altar — a primitive stone table and an upright stone column — a massebe — was where Jacob would sacrifice on the morrow. There he planned to pray and sleep until the Lord gave direction concerning his journey to Egypt.

Before the sun rose, leaning on Judah's arm, with his other sons accompanying him, he walked to the sacred tree. On his shoulders, Benjamin carried an unblemished yearling lamb for the sacrifice. Other sons carried wood and fire-making materials. Soon a fire roared in the firepit blackened by centuries of sacrificial fires. Jacob, tall and straight in spite of his more than one hundred years, stood reverently before the altar. Benjamin gently laid the lamb before him.

Jacob thought of the story his father, Isaac, had often told of traveling with his father, Abraham, to the sacred mountain and there finding himself lying on the altar of sacrifice with his father holding the sacrificial knife above him. He sighed and looked at his sons. He took Benjamin's hands in his. "My sons, I have told you often of my father's experience on the mount. There is a great lesson to be learned from that experience. Sometimes," he said, "God clearly directs. Other times He merely permits some things to happen. Therefore, we will not always understand the role of God's hand, but we know enough of his heart and mind to be submissive."

Benjamin nodded. He had heard the story often of Abraham and

Isaac, and the providing of the sacrificial ram.

Jacob released Benjamin's hand, closed his near-sightless eyes, and prayed: "God of my fathers, Abraham and Isaac, be with me now as you were with them. Just as you provided the sacrificial ram for Abraham, provide me with answers to my prayers." With a deft twist of his wrist, he slit the yielding throat of the lamb. Judah stood ready with a cup, catching the blood as it ran freely from the severed vessels. "God of Abraham and Isaac, accept this sacrifice from our hand," Jacob intoned, "that our lives might be sanctified before Thee." He stepped back from the altar.

Benjamin picked up the lamb and placed it whole on the brightly burning fire.

Jacob took the proffered cup of blood from Judah, sprinkling blood over the altar, then on his own clothes. Motioning for his sons to leave him, he sat down next to the altar, his back against the sacred tree. The flickering sacrificial fire lighted his face. Black clouds of smoke rose to the heavens.

For three nights, Jacob sat under the sacred tree. He prayed continuously for the Lord's assurance that it was right that he take his family to Egypt.

On the third night an answer came. God spoke to him in a solemn voice. "Jacob. Jacob."

Instantly awake, Jacob answered. "Here am I."

"Jacob, I am the God of your fathers. Fear not to go down to Egypt. I will there make of you a great nation. I will go down with you into Egypt and I will also surely bring you up again; and Joseph shall put his hand upon your eyes."

Jacob bowed low and touched his face to the dirt before the sacred tree. Tears streaked down his dusty cheeks, running into his matted white beard. His heart was satisfied. Most pleasing of all to him was God's promise that Joseph would put his hands upon his eyes! The expression signified that Joseph would protect him and care for him in his old age among the heathen. Tears flowed as he realized it also meant that Joseph would be the one who would close his eyes at the time of his death. Next morning the strengthened Jacob made ready to proceed to Egypt. His sons and their wives struck the tent city and rapidly loaded the waiting carts. They lifted Jacob into the elegant Egyptian carrying chair lashed to the backs of two white asses.

Seventeen days of desert crossing passed without event. Soon they arrived at the border fortress of Thel. Though Jacob still had reservations about living in the land of Egypt, his people happily sang as they rode. They came to the gate — the way leading to Joseph's kingdom. Pharaoh's border guards had been informed of the coming of Jacob and his family. Their orders came from Pharaoh himself: Treat these immigrants with respect! So, instead of the usual brusqueness, they smiled politely. They bowed low before Pharaoh's insignia on wagons and on the carrying chair of the aged Jacob.

A smiling Egyptian stepped forward and saluted the brothers. "I am Aures," he said, rubbing his hands together in apparent anticipation. "I bring you greetings of the Pharaoh. He bids you welcome. The grand vizier assigned me to guide you into Kemet, the black land." Aures smiled and bowed before Jacob.

He signaled the gate guard. Bronze gratings swung open. Jacob's people passed through with wagons and flocks. They halted at noon. His sons lifted Jacob's litter down from the asses' backs. "Here you will wait, your lordship," said Aures. "I will take one of your sons with me to fetch your son and my master, the Grand Vizier of Egypt."

"Yes," breathed Jacob. "Tell my son we have arrived."

Aures left, accompanied by Judah.

The place where Jacob waited was a charming spot. Three palm trees, growing as it seemed from one root, shaded Jacob. The air remained cool, a welcome contrast from the interminable desert heat through which they had traveled. Jacob sat immobile, patient, surrounded by his sons. A little pool with blue and rose colored lotus blossoms sparkled at his feet. The land of Goshen lay before him: scattered clumps of trees, ditches lined with tall reeds, plowed fields, open meadows, pastureland and small villages. Birds flew overhead. Jacob's old eyes looked far out across the expanse, seeing little of the earthly scenery before him. What he saw was greater.

There was a stir in the far ranks of the assembled people, then a whisper which soon became a babble. Necks craned. Coming towards them, led by Aures and Judah, was a gold-plated chariot pulled by two white horses straining at their bits. A path cleared through the crowd. As the chariot stopped, an eager youth stepped forward and grabbed the reins of the beautiful chargers. A man, blue-eyed and tall, stepped down from the chariot and walked toward the old man sitting under the palm trees. He knelt before him, took the old wrinkled hands and brought them reverently to his lips. "Father, it is I, your son, Joseph."

Chapter 19: People of the Covenant

"Father, do you forgive me?" Joseph asked. He and his father sat on stools before Jacob's goat-hair tent. Bread, cheese, and goat's milk, which a servant had brought for their lunch, sat untouched. From where they sat, they could see tents of the entire tribe pitched amidst Goshen's verdant green.

Watching his father closely, Joseph waited for his answer. He hoped his father would realize that, in his question, he pleaded forgiveness for many things: for childish arrogance, for blind conceit, for a neglect of more than twenty years.

Jacob rose slowly to his feet. Joseph stood with him. His father laid a quavering hand on each of his shoulders, then looked at him intently. "There is no need of forgiveness, for there has been no sin," he said. Then he looked at the brassy heavens. "God is merciful," he added. "For he has given my son back to me. For that, I can now die happy."

Joseph drew his father to him a gentle embrace. They stood without moving until the sharp noise of someone clearing his throat roused them. Joseph raised moist eyes.

Reuben stood before them. He cleared his throat again. "The family members desire to meet their illustrious relative," he said with a grin. He motioned. The people assembled at the tent area's far edge came forward to meet Joseph. They seemed shy of this tall, blond stranger who wore bracelets on his arms and a gold chain around his neck. Reuben stood beside Joseph, naming names of each family member. Other than his brothers, Joseph saw no familiar faces, but he spoke cordially to everyone.

Squinting in his attempt to make out faces of his grandchildren and great-grandchildren, Jacob nodded to each.

Following introductions, Joseph spoke. "You are now in the land of Goshen, Pharaoh's beautiful pastureland. Pharaoh himself granted permission for you to stay here. This is Egypt, but here in Goshen things are not very Egyptian. You shall live here as free as you did in Mamre." He spread his arms, encompassing the fields before him. "Here you may graze your flocks. Here your herds will prosper. Here you may erect tents and homes of brick in which to live with your families." He turned to Jacob. "Father, here the One God's promise of a chosen generation will come true." He stepped back and put an arm across his father's bony shoulder. "I have arranged for a house to be built for you."

Jacob shook his head. "No, my son." He closed his eyes and smiled.

Then he looked up. "My tent has always been my home. It will be my home until I die."

"As you desire." Joseph squeezed his father's shoulder. He turned back to the tribe spread out before him. "It is important that you get along with the Egyptian people. You are different, with different manners, different beliefs, different gods. Yet, I ask you to respect the people who are here. They are your neighbors. Do not antagonize them." He smiled at the silent throng. "All Pharaoh asks is that you respect their beliefs as they will respect yours."

He turned from the people. Motioning to Reuben, he said, "Please have all the brothers meet me in father's tent." He helped Jacob into the dim confines of the tent, seated him on the cushions of his bed, then waited for the brothers. When all were assembled, he smiled. "Again I greet you in love. It has been a good day." He looked down at the dozing Jacob. "It is good to see my father once more. Now I will go to the Pharaoh, return his wagons and asses, and tell him that my father's entire household has arrived safely in the land of Egypt."

He looked piercingly at each of the brothers. "It is important that Pharaoh not be threatened by your presence. If he felt you were warriors, it might be detrimental. I told him you are shepherds and herdsmen, that you brought your flocks and herds with you. Pharaoh expressed a desire to meet my brothers. I cannot take all of you this time. Some will have to remain and complete unpacking and arranging your tents. He looked at them, evaluating them. "Reuben, I would like you to go with me and Issachar, and Judah, and Zebulon." He paused before continuing, weighing something in his mind. Then he looked at his younger brother. "And Benjamin. I would like you to accompany me, also."

Those who had been chosen seemed pleased. Several others grumbled a little, but accepted Joseph's decision. He continued, "When you are before Pharaoh, he will ask you about your occupations. It is important to show him respect, for he is the king of this entire land. In your answer, tell him the truth, that your trade has been working with cattle since your youth."

Simeon growled, "Why all this attention to our ability to take care of cattle?"

Joseph fixed him with a cold square. "Someone told Pharaoh about the destruction of Shechem. He is concerned that you may be soldiers preparing to breed insurrection in his land. That, he will not tolerate. If you are herders, he is willing that you dwell here in Goshen." He smiled wryly. "Besides," he said, "Egyptians look down upon shepherds. As shepherds, you will be an abomination to the Egyptians. Therefore, you will not be disturbed."

He knelt before Jacob. "Father, I must go now. I will return next week with my wife, Asenath, and your grandchildren, Manasseh and Ephraim. Then, after you have rested, I will present you to Pharaoh."

Jacob nodded. "Go in peace, my son."

He spoke to the brothers he had chosen to accompany him to see Pharaoh. "Normally, I would have you go by boat to see Pharaoh at Avaris, but the river is too low. I will send Amunebet to guide you overland to the royal city. There I will meet you day after tomorrow." He kissed his father on both cheeks and strode from the tent. Mounting his chariot, he wheeled his glistening white stallions and was soon seen as nothing but a cloud of dust in the distance.

* * *

Two days later, Joseph and five brothers stood before Pharaoh, surrounded by palace officials. Joseph bowed low to the floor, his brothers following his example. He had a hard time getting them to pay attention. They had never seen such finery, nor been in such a hall.

The great king nodded. "You may speak, Joseph."

Joseph bowed again. "Mighty King, my brethren and my father's household, together with flocks and cattle, have come from the land of Canaan to sojourn in Egypt."

Pharaoh sat silently, his chin cupped in his hand, one elbow resting on his knee, eyes roving from one brother to another.

Several of the brothers fidgeted nervously under his gaze. Pharaoh pointed a bejeweled finger at Judah. "What is your occupation?"

Judah, following the lead of Joseph, bowed his head, then answered, "We are shepherds. Both we and our fathers before us."

The answer seemed to please Pharaoh. He smiled at Joseph. "Place your father and your brothers in the best part of the land. Give them whatsoever they desire."

"I have placed them in the land of Goshen. I request that you let them remain in Goshen where their tents are already pitched. There they can feed their flocks apart from the Egyptians."

"It is done." Pharaoh waved his hand as if the matter were a triviality. Then he looked quizzically at Joseph. "Why have you not brought your father to me?"

Joseph bowed again. "My father is very old, my king. He is tired from the journey. If you desire, I will bring him to you as soon as he is rested."

"It is my desire." The Pharaoh seemed ready to dismiss the brothers, but then turned to Benjamin. "Is this the younger brother you told me about?"

"Yes, my king."

He motioned Benjamin forward. "Have you also been a shepherd all your life?"

"Yes, your highness."

"Do you understand the breeding and raising of cattle?"

Benjamin looked him in the face. "That has been our life, O Pharaoh. That is what we know best. We have come to Egypt because there are no longer pastures for our flocks in Canaan."

"I am delighted," Pharaoh said. "Joseph, assign your brothers as official keepers of my personal cattle herds in Goshen." He turned to a scribe who sat near his feet. "Make up a document making Joseph's father and his family legal tenants in the Land of Goshen. Then make up a second contract assigning them as my official herdsmen."

"Thank you, great king. We will return. In ten days I will bring my father before you."

Again, Pharaoh nodded his acceptance. Joseph bowed to the palace courtiers, then led his brothers from the chamber.

True to his word, Joseph returned to the Pharaoh with his venerable father. Jacob made a stately entrance into the great palace. Pharaoh and Jacob looked at each other: the old man, patriarch to his family; the young king, ruler of all Egypt. Jacob did not bow. Joseph, one step behind his father, smiled and winked at Pharaoh.

The Pharaoh broke the silence. To Jacob, he said, "You have begot a son whom Pharaoh loves. He is a leader of men. None is greater in the land of Egypt, save myself."

Jacob said simply, "He is son of a king, grandson of a king, and great-grandson of a king. Kingship is his birthright."

Pharaoh raised his eyebrows. "Son of a king?"

Jacob straightened his old body. He looked firmly into the eyes of the Pharaoh. "Yes, King of Egypt. Son of a King. He is also a son of God." "I do not understand," Pharaoh said as he leaned forward. "How can he be the son of God? In Egypt, Pharaoh is the son of the god, Osiris. Who is this God of whom Joseph is son?"

Fixing his eyes on Pharaoh's face, Jacob replied, "There is only one

God. He is the God of my fathers, Abraham and Isaac. He it is who created this world. He created all mankind as his children — his sons and daughters."

Pharaoh smiled indulgently at the ancient patriarch. "We welcome you, your family, and your god to Egypt."

Leaning on Joseph's arm, Jacob leaned forward until he almost touched the untouchable Pharaoh. His eyes twinkled as he said, "I bless you, most royal Pharaoh. In the name of the One God, I bless you with health and continued prosperity. May your life be long in this land."

Pharaoh laid his hand on Jacob's arm. "Father of Joseph, how old are you?"

"The years of my life are an hundred and thirty. It has been a full life, but with its share of evil. Even as old as I am, I have not yet lived as long as did my father, or even his father." He bowed before the young monarch and shuffled from the hall. Joseph bowed before his king and followed his father.

Jacob leaned against a tent post. Almost completely blind, only Joseph's voice gave him indication of where to focus.

"Father," Joseph asked. "Is there anything else I can do for you?"

Breathing deeply, Jacob let his sightless eyes roam around the tent. He knew its every shadow and space. To him it was a familiar and comfortable place. "My son, there needs to be a record kept of our family. A genealogy. A record which will tell future generations of God's dealings with the seed of Abraham."

Joseph smiled and placed a roll of papyrus in the hands of Jacob. "Father, this is a journal I have kept. It contains a record of all God's dealings with me from the time I left Canaan until now."

Bowing his head, Jacob said, "Praise the Lord. There shall be a record preserved of our people." He looked up. "But will the papyrus last through the necessary generations?"

Again Joseph smiled. "Father, I have transcribed my writings onto bronze plates. They will last forever. They will be a record of your people that future generations will look to and remember us by."

Jacob nodded his pleasure. "So be it."

"Father?" Joseph said hesitantly.

"What, my son?"

"The record is only of God's dealings with me. I want to know of God's dealings with you and our people." He paused for emphasis. "I want to write the history of our people from the creation of the earth down to the present."

Again Jacob nodded. "It shall be the work of my old age." He cradled the papyrus to his breast.

Each time Joseph visited his father, he brought his scribe materials. He sat on the floor of the tent at Jacob's feet. As Jacob told the creation story, told of the flood, of Abraham and Isaac, Joseph wrote with brushes on the rolls of papyrus. Jacob recounted legends handed down from father to son for generations. He told Joseph of Abraham's visit with the aged Shem, son of Noah. Carefully, he recited the royal lineage of the family back to Adam, the first man. From his father, Isaac, he had heard the stories. He passed those stories on to Joseph. They discussed their relationship to the One God. "Mortal life has a purpose," Jacob said. "Sometimes we do not know His purposes, but we do know He loves us."

"That is a powerful idea," Joseph said.

"Yes," Israel mused. "The eternal truth that our Heavenly Father loves all his children is an immensely powerful idea." He paused.

Joseph waited patiently.

"Love is the most powerful force in the world," Israel said. "It is a driving force. It is something that carries us through our life of joyful duty."

"What purpose do you think the One God had in bringing your family to Egypt?" Joseph asked.

Israel shrugged. "That I do not fully know. But He has revealed to me that there are going to be dark days for our people. The time will come when there will be a Pharaoh who does not know Joseph." He looked at his son through sightless eyes. "Through it all, remember the word of the One God: 'I will bring my people forth once again from Egypt. They shall yet inherit the land of their fathers.'"

Chapter 20: Man of Wisdom

Joseph, in his weekly meeting with the Pharaoh, predicted that the rains would soon fall in the south, the Nile would again run full. Runners from the palace traveled to all Egypt's major cities with the exciting proclamation. "The grand vizier says the famine is over." Tears of joy ran freely as people heard the news. "The famine is over!" From northern delta to southern desert rang the cry.

As Joseph prophesied, the trickle in the riverbed began to swell, at first almost imperceptibly, then each day more and more until with a joyous gush of swift, silt-laden water, the river revived. People put off their long faces and feasted in the streets. Fishermen launched their boats. Like butterfly wings in early spring, the Nile again bloomed with brightly-colored sails. Dry canals, cleaned and strengthened under Joseph's leadership, opened to admit the fertile flood. Farmers planted precious seeds, hoarded for seven years. Temples of Egypt, het-natjer, swelled as people thronged to them to offer sacrifices and give thanks. From the delta where the Nile met the great sea to the second cataract in the highlands, the land belonged to Pharaoh. Joseph's assistants collected the tax of one-fifth of each harvest. Rumors reached Joseph that Pharaoh's advisors felt more tax should be assessed to care for the poor. Amenhotep called Joseph to the palace.

He knew what the issue would be. A hush fell on the crowd surrounding the throne as Joseph arrived in the great hall. He walked slowly past the guards, bowed low before the Pharaoh and Queen Kemsiyet. Straightening, he faced his ruler.

Pharaoh leaned toward Joseph. "My advisors tell me that taxes need to be raised to make sure the poor are fed and cared for."

Joseph looked at the king's advisors. They could not meet his gaze, but dropped their eyes. He spoke directly to Pharaoh. "My king, your advisors are right in the sense that we must meet the people's needs. I know of your concern, so let me speak in parable. During the years of plenty, our fishing fleets were the mightiest of the great sea. Ships returned with full tanks. Pelicans and gulls filled their bellies from offal cast overboard. No longer did birds need to fish for themselves. There was abundance. Then came famine. The river dried up. Our fishing fleet was grounded. Fish were still plentiful in the great sea, but the birds, now dependent upon free handouts, had forgotten how to fish. They died by the thousands."

He looked around at the attentive faces, then returned his attention to

Pharaoh. "In the country of my youth, Canaanites are very experienced with predators which would kill their sheep. Herders plant razor-sharp bronze knives handle down in the ground, then coat the blades with sheep blood. Wolves and lions smell the blood, lick the knives, and cut their tongues. This brings a seemingly inexhaustible supply of good, warm blood, free and without effort. Wolves lick their own blood until they die." Joseph looked again at the court advisors. "It would be easy to provide all the needs of our people. But by so doing, we put them in the same position of the gulls and pelicans. Welfare creates a weak, dependent people and a weak nation, unable to sustain itself. Like the predators of Canaan, when we tax the people heavily to give them back welfare programs, they become like the wolves and lions. They would feed on their own blood, and the results would be equally disastrous. The country would die." He bowed low before Pharaoh. "My king, the tax we have instituted in Egypt is fair and sufficient to care for needs of those who cannot provide for themselves, without becoming oppressive to those who pay."

Pharaoh nodded. In a quiet but firm voice he announced to the court, "Joseph, the grand vizier, has spoken. His decision shall stand." He dismissed the scribes and courtiers. Joseph stood alone before the royal pair. He bowed slightly before Kemsiyet, the queen, who smiled.

Amenhotep motioned Joseph forward. They clasped hands. "Thank you again for saving Egypt and for making Pharaoh wealthy beyond measure."

Joseph lowered his eyes respectfully. "My king, God used you to give me my freedom. Otherwise, I might still be in the royal prison with my family starving in Canaan."

Nodding good-naturedly, Amenhotep said, "If your God had left you in prison, that would have been a serious mistake."

Joseph smiled back, knowing Pharaoh was in a philosophical mood. "My God does not make mistakes. It is only when men treat themselves as mistakes that they become mistakes."

"You have told me that man has the power to choose."

"That is what I believe. God gives us power to choose for ourselves. It is our greatest power."

Pharaoh asked, "Did you choose to release yourself from prison?" He waited expectantly for Joseph's answer.

"I believe I did, in a way," Joseph answered with a smile. "Attitude certainly helped."

The queen looked puzzled. "I do not understand."

Joseph sat on the stoop before her. "Some people, especially those who are weak, when faced with adversity such as crop failure, or being thrown into prison, give up and whine about their bad luck. I believe God permits us to be knocked down only when there is opportunity to grow. We have a choice, we can either get up, or we can stay down. But, if we stay down, we lose the opportunity. If we endure well the adversity, we can grasp opportunity and go forward in accomplishment." He thought for a moment, wanting to come up with just the right analogy. "On my estate, I must prune the trees if I want a good fruit crop. I believe God prunes us when He wants us to grow."

The queen leaned forward, obviously thinking about what he had said. Joseph continued. "The real tragedies in life are those people who never accomplish what God intends them to accomplish. When faced with adversity they just lie down and quit."

Kemsiyet still seemed unsatisfied. She asked. "What motivates people to keep on — to rise above adversity?"

Amenhotep sat up with a start. "It's the dream! The mountains of the King — the pyramids. That is the key. Without a dream — a desire — the pyramids would not have been built. Without dreams, there would be no temples, no palaces, no pyramids." He pursed his lips. "If that is true, every monument of mankind is based on a dream!" He looked triumphantly at Joseph.

"My king," Joseph said. "You should have been a philosopher!"

* * *

Dangling his feet in the water of the lily pool, Ephraim sat glumly thinking. He was not aware of anyone near until he felt a hand on his shoulder. Turning, he looked up at his father, seeing concern in his father's eyes.

Ephraim, eleven, seemed short for his age, but stocky and strongly built. His chest promised one day to be powerful. A bold, arching nose dominated his face but did not detract from pale, brooding eyes. His shy mouth gave him a look both intense and thoughtful. A leather thong around his forehead bound reddish-blonde hair, hanging straight to his shoulders. He wore a short, vividly embroidered tunic which exposed bronzed legs and arms. He turned back to the pond, slowly kicking his feet in the water.

"Something troubles you, son?"

Ephraim shook his head, afraid tears would flow if he answered.

Joseph sat next to him on the tile, hands clasped, his knees up to his chin.

Without turning, Ephraim broke the silence. "Father, why did God punish me by giving me a crippled foot?"

His father did not answer immediately and Ephraim continued somewhat bitterly. "Look at Manasseh and Tem. They run and fight like real soldiers. All I can do is limp after them." He punctuated his sentence by splashing his feed savagely in the water.

Gently, Joseph asked, "Ephraim, is it possible that God has purposes for you that do not include running and fighting?"

Ephraim turned, his brow wrinkled. "But father, that is what I want to do."

Joseph reached to help Ephraim, who shrugged off the proffered hand and pulled himself to his feet.

Joseph said, "Son, come with me. I would like you to see something." They walked side by side to the stables. The team of albino horses snorted eagerly. They seemed anxious to run. The stable boy was not to be seen, so Joseph quickly harnessed the team. He stepped into the chariot and motioned Ephraim to get in with him.

They did not attempt to speak as the chariot rattled noisily over the rutted road to On. They stopped just short of the market place. Joseph gave the reins to a ragged urchin, dropping a copper coin into the outstretched hand, then they started through the streets. Ephraim had to limp fast to keep up. Every once in awhile he looked up at his famous father. People moved out of their way. Those that recognized Joseph bowed and shouted praises.

In the market, they heard the usual morning clatter as beggars and peddlers set up shop for the day. Folding stools rattled open, covered baskets filled with squawking fowl stood beside overflowing tables. Along the walls men and women spread their mats and arranged their wares, accompanied by constant gossip or loud bursts of laughter. Everywhere white shentis fluttered, brown arms stretched and flexed, gleaming backs bent. It was market day in On.

Ephraim followed his father into a street lined with fish stalls. The pavement was slippery with refuse, and crowded with noisy humanity. Ephraim gagged at the stink. They threaded their way through the crowd, stumbling over scavenging dogs, dodging beggars who clutched at their garments and whined after them. They avoided ubiquitous urchins who dashed this way and that under their feet, fighting savagely for bits of bread. Strings of dried fish hung everywhere — fish surrounded by clouds of flies which flew off as people passed, then settled again. Flies' buzzing added a lazy note to the ever-present din.

They stopped at a basketmaker's stall. An old man sat on a reed mat, a blanket thrown loosely over his legs. His hands deftly guided reeds in an out of the basket he was making, almost quicker than the eye could follow. His wares hung all over the stall — baskets of all shapes and sizes — inviting people to buy them. The basket maker was naked to the waist. A blanket covered him from the waist down. Angry purple scars laced his chest and abdomen. Sensing their presence, he stopped weaving and looked up expectantly.

Joseph spoke softly. "Hello, Khyan."

A broad smile lighted the basketmaker's face. He reached up with his hand. Joseph took it, clasping it warmly. "Joseph, my friend. It is good to see you again."

"Khyan, I have come to buy some baskets. My son, Ephraim, is with me." The basketmaker smiled again, and held out his hands. "Your son. Let me see him."

Joseph guided the reluctant Ephraim forwards toward the outstretched hands.

Khyan grasped Ephraim, pulling him down. Then methodically, he ran his roughened hands all over the young body. Ephraim, frightened, looked at his father. Joseph smiled reassuringly.

"He is a fine boy," said Khyan. "Athletic and well-muscled."

"Yes, my friend," Joseph answered, "but he has a defect. He was born with a club foot. He walks with a limp."

Ephraim jumped as Khyan burst into a cackle of laughter, slapping his side. "A defect, you say!" He continued weaving the basket as he laughed.

Ephraim looked again at Joseph, a question in his wide eyes.

Khyan stopped laughing, suddenly becoming serious. He spoke forcefully. "Is the defect a handicap?" he asked, then answered his own question. "Listen to an old man, my son, and listen carefully." He raised a gnarled hand and pointed it at Ephraim. "A defect is only a handicap when we think it to be one."

Ephraim was not sure how to accept that statement. He tried to understand. Was he being made fun of? His hands balled into fists. Khyan was still talking. "My son, sometimes trouble is the best thing that ever happens to us. Eliminate our problems and we would be weak and worthless. God gives us problems to make us strong." He paused, rubbing his sightless eyes. Then he cackled again. "My boy, a smooth sea never made a skillful sailor." He lapsed into silence.

Joseph said, "Thank you for your wisdom, Khyan. I will take one of your medium baskets." He placed several coins in a cup at Khyan's side, then pulled Ephraim out of the stall and back into the street.

They walked quietly back the way they had come until Joseph stopped Ephraim in front of a beggar who sat against the wall. The beggar, dirty and unkempt, wailed loudly. When he saw wealthy-looking Joseph, his wails increased. Joseph stopped and dropped several coins into the dirty, outstretched hand.

Instead of returning to the chariot, Joseph led Ephraim into a side street which led to a small temple inside a hedge of old sycamore trees. Its pylons were thick with images, its courts shaded by awnings. Colorful halls were simple but spacious. Picture writing covered its walls. Joseph led Ephraim to one wall, stopped, and asked him to read aloud what was written.

Ephraim read the hieroglyphics haltingly: "It takes courage to achieve in life. It is not as important that you go into battle expecting to win — as to just go into battled determined not to lose."

Without a word, Joseph wheeled his young son and started back though the marketplace. Neither spoke until they were in the chariot. Ephraim looked up. "Father, what does it all mean?"

Joseph did not answer, but drove silently. Near the Nile he stopped, helped Ephraim out, and guided him to the river bank where they sat. It was night. A warm wind blew off the river from the north, carrying suggestion of swamps and dampness. The sky was clear. Stars gave enough light for them to see trees lining the river.

"My son, I think I understand how you feel. It is not fun to be different from other boys. I hurts when some tease you about your crooked foot." Joseph paused. He had difficulty putting his feelings into words. He paused, then continued. "What did you think of Khyan?" Ephraim shrugged. "He seemed like a nice old man, but I did not understand what he meant."

"Did you notice his eyes?"

"I couldn't see his eyes. He looked sort of funny and acted like he couldn't see."

"He is totally blind. The Assyrians captured him and gouged out his eyes. Did you notice his legs?"

"No, father. They were covered by a blanket."

"Khyan does that so as to not attract attention to them. He has no legs, Ephraim. The Assyrians tortured him, then cut off his legs."

"No eyes? No legs?" Shock sounded through Ephraim's words. He remembered also the criss-crossed purple scars on Khyan's chest.

Joseph plucked a long stalk of grass from beside him and chewed on it silently. Then once again he spoke. "Did you notice the beggar to whom I gave alms?"

Ephraim shuddered and wrinkled his nose. "Yes. He was dirty and even smelled."

"Did you see anything wrong with him?"

"He had a patch over one eye."

"Is that all?"

Ephraim looked up at his father in the light of the stars. "That is all I noticed, Father."

Joseph drew his knees up, chewed on the stem of grass, and looked across the broad river. As he looked, the river gave him an idea. He spoke softly, so that Ephraim had to listen carefully to hear his words. "Son, there are all kinds of people in the world. Some, like the beggar we saw, accomplish nothing. They are leeches who won't work but live off the labor of others." He spit out the grass stalk and looked again at the river. "They are people who never seem to get their feet wet in the river of life."

"A second group of people go through life hardly seen or recognized. They just seem to float downstream, taking the path of least resistance. They lean on others for assistance, but do contribute something to humanity. "The third group, son, are made up of people like my friend, Khyan. They are leaders. They strive forward, never complaining. They accomplish great things with next to nothing. They are willing to fight the current, to go upstream." He paused reflectively. "Son, the only difference between the beggar and Khyan is their attitude. The beggar has nothing wrong with him. He just chooses to beg. Khyan, by all rights, should be a beggar, but he is a producer. He earns his own way. He will not accept charity."

Joseph faced Ephraim in the starlight. "My son, your attitude, not any particular physical feature, will determine your future." He paused again to collect his thoughts. "In my own life I have found that the greater the difficulty, the greater the opportunity." He thought back over his slavery and imprisonment, then looked up once more. "Ephraim, I have seen more men blessed through handicap and adversity than have been perfected through health and prosperity."

He reached over and pulled Ephraim to him. Then he said gently. "Ephraim, the decision of what you will be in life is entirely up to you. You can be a man of strength and courage like Khyan. Or you can use your limp as an excuse to become like the beggar. Which will it be?"

Ephraim threw his arms around his father's neck. "Oh, Father. I don't want to be a beggar. I want to be like you."

Joseph's eyes misted, then tears ran freely down his cheeks.

Chapter 21: Death of Jacob

Each year the Nile flooded and receded, flooded and receded, back on its regular schedule. Its constancy lulled people again into a feeling of security. They soon forgot famine and its attendant discomforts. Joseph kept busy governing Egypt, thankful that Manasseh and Ephraim now carried part of that responsibility. Manasseh, twenty-four, no longer lived at home. Tall and dark, he had his mother's dark, flashing eyes. A born leader, he had become Joseph's chief administrator, traveling to Egypt's far-flung cities to supervise collection of taxes, manage the work projects, and obtain accurate measurements during the river's annual cycles.

Ephraim at twenty-one — a happy and rather modest young man — still lived on Joseph's estate. Since his ninth birthday he had been enrolled in the king's school where he learned to write Egyptian hieroglyphics. In addition to committing over seven hundred characters to memory, he also excelled in bookkeeping, mathematics, and astronomy. Honor student in the school of the scribes, he surpassed all others in his depth of knowledge and ornateness of writing. As a follow-up to Ephraim's scribe training, Joseph employed Gershon, son of Levi, to instruct Ephraim in the ancient language of the patriarchs. Ephraim, fluent in both written languages, served as chief scribe for Joseph, working closely with him in all affairs of the kingdom. With his fair hair, eyes, and skin, he seemed out of place among the Egyptians with whom he worked.

Joseph's family had matured. Asenath, always graceful and beautiful, had ripened to a stately elegance. Gray silvered her dark hair, but her olive complexion remained unwrinkled. Three more children graced the halls and gardens of the estate. Rachel, a regal beauty at sixteen, had the queenly bearing of her mother and the stately demeanor of Joseph. Her temper erupted quickly, but repentance was also quick. She occupied her time learning to dance.

Osnath, their second girl, was almost the opposite of Rachel. Quiet and sedate, she displayed a kindness that reminded Joseph of his own youth. She loved small animals and nursed several lamed birds back to health. Their youngest child, Rebecca, named after her great-grandmother, was a playful child of ten — the very likeness of the child, Asenath. Rebecca had a way of getting her father to do just what she wanted.

One afternoon Joseph and Rebecca played in the backyard, only to be interrupted by Amunebet. "Sir, one of your brothers is here." Joseph straightened quickly. What could it be was Jacob. . .?

He excused himself to Rebecca and hurried from the house. Napthali, son of the maid, Bilhah, waited for him, clad in a white, belted smock almost covered by his great, gray beard. Joseph calculated Napthali must be close to sixty-five years of age. His beard-covered, lean, angular face contrasted sharply with his shiny bald head.

"What is it?" Joseph asked, as they grasped hands.

"Father sent for you. He begs you to come quickly."

"Is he . . . ?"

"At one hundred and forty-seven years?"

He signaled Amunebet. "Prepare two chariots. Rouse Ephraim. Send word to Manasseh. We go to Heliopolis in Goshen." While his chariot was prepared, Joseph took time only to say goodbye to Asenath and the girls.

When they arrived, Jacob appeared to be dozing. Fever flushed his cheeks. His breath came in short gasps. He lay propped up in bed to aid his breathing, but his complexion remained gray. Joseph, careful not to disturb his father, moved close to the bed.

Without opening his eyes, Jacob asked, "Is that you, Joseph?"

"Yes, father."

"It is good that you came," Jacob sighed. "I am old and weak. My life is nearly done." He motioned with his arm. "Come, take a stool here beside me."

Joseph sat beside the bed and took one of his father's cold hands in his. In a comforting voice, he said, "Father, do not talk now. I will stay here with you."

Jacob, eyes closed, shook his head. "It is important that I talk. I die soon. The God of your ancestors showed me that he will bring back our people to the land He promised us. Therefore, when I am dead, bury me in the cave in Machpelach, in the land of Canaan, near my ancestors."

Squeezing his father's hand, Joseph pledged, "My father, I promise you that you shall be carried to the tomb in Machpelach."

Jacob sighed, then leaned over and let his head rest on Joseph's shoulder.

Joseph carefully laid his father on the bed, then knelt beside his father's bed and touched his forehead to the carpet. Jacob asked weakly, "Joseph?"

"I am here, father."

"Oh, my son," whispered Jacob. "I knew you would come." A

servant straightened the leopard fur drawn over his bony knees. He slipped back into sleep.

Joseph was glad he had conversed so extensively during his father's seventeen years in Egypt, glad for stories, genealogy, and experiences Jacob told him. All had been inscribed on the bronze plates. Jacob's posterity would have a knowledge of this great man.

Jacob's eyes opened. "Are you still here, Joseph?"

"Yes, father." Joseph took his hand. "Manasseh and Ephraim are with me."

"I prayed they would accompany you. The God of my fathers shall bless them. They shall be called after my name, Israel. The children you have after these two shall be yours, but these two are mine. Their tribes shall be called the tribes of Manasseh and of Ephraim." Jacob coughed and his body shuddered, but he continued. "Before I die, I desire to testify to you that God appeared to me at Luz in the land of Canaan, and blessed me. He told me He would make me fruitful, and multiply me, and make of me a multitude of people."

He coughed, his mouth dry. The servant held a glass to his lips. He waved it away and continued. "He promised me he would give that land to my seed for an everlasting possession." He coughed again. "Joseph, God raised you up to save my house from death. Because you have delivered our people from the famine which was sore in the land, God shall bless you and the fruit of your loins. Your two sons shall be blessed above your brothers, and ever above your father's house." He paused as he fought for breath. "Your father's house bowed down before you as shown you in your dreams." He lay back. After resting, he said, "Help me to sit. I would see your sons." Joseph helped his father as he struggled to hang his emaciated legs over the side of the bed.

Stepping out of the tent, Joseph called Manasseh and Ephraim. They entered the tent and greeted their grandfather respectfully. The sightless old eyes looked at where the young men stood. "My grandsons, I am dying. The Lord made known to me that you are part of my blessing. You will inherit the promised land. It is you who will be fruitful and become a multitude of people." Expressing his urgency, he spoke to Joseph, "My son, listen carefully."

Joseph leaned closer.

"Your sons, Ephraim and Manasseh, shall replace Reuben and Simeon in my blessings."

A look of shock passed over Joseph's face. His sons, Manasseh and

Ephraim, would be counted as Jacob's own sons.

"They shall be part of the inheritance and will have their place in the promised land. Bring them to me."

Joseph guided the two young men forward, until Jacob's grasping hands could touch them. As he embraced them, his tears left wet smudges on their cheeks.

"Guide my hands to their heads. I would bless them."

Quickly directing the boys to kneel before their grandfather, Joseph placed Jacob's right hand on the head of Manasseh, the first born, and the left hand on Ephraim.

Jacob said, "My son, I had given up ever again seeing your face. Now I see not only your face, but also the faces of your children." His gaze was towards the heavens, and it seemed to Joseph that his father's face glowed with a heavenly aura.

To Joseph's great surprise, Jacob lifted his hands from the heads of his kneeling grandsons, then crossed them so the right hand was on the head of Ephraim. He began his blessing: "Oh, God in heaven — that same God before whom my fathers Abraham and Isaac did walk, the God who has fed me all my life until this day — bless these Thy sons with Thy choicest blessings. And let my name be named on them, and the name of my fathers, Abraham and Isaac. Bless each of them that they may be a great people, but I bless him upon whom my right hand rests to become a multitude of nations."

He was continuing, but Joseph interrupted him. "Father, you have made a mistake." He lifted Jacob's right hand and placed it back on Manasseh. "This is the firstborn."

The old man switched hands again. "I know, son. The Lord told me the youngest shall carry the blessing. Do not be saddened. This one," he raised his left hand from Manasseh's head, "shall also become a people, and shall be great, but truly his younger brother shall be greater, and his seed shall become a multitude of nations." When he finished the blessings, Jacob motioned Joseph to him. "Almost whispering, he said, "When we lived near Shechem, I bought a small plot of ground." He reached out with his bony hand, clasping Joseph's hand. "I fought for that ground. When I die I want you to have it." He silenced Joseph's protest. "Joseph, though I die, God will be with you and will once again bring you back to the land of your fathers." He dropped Joseph's hand and lay back on the pillow. "I need to be dressed before you bring your brothers."

Joseph summoned the servants. They dressed Jacob in his patriarchal robe. He sat on the edge of the bed, supported by his servants, his bearing regal. His hair, white and thin, framed his face. His full lustrous white beard hung almost to his waist. Joseph took his hand, then kissed him on the forehead.

"Bring in your brothers," Jacob whispered. "I would give them my blessings."

Joseph summoned the brothers. They trooped into the tent, concern on their faces. Joseph whispered to his father that they were there, then whispered to Ephraim. "Do you have papyrus and ink?"

"Yes, father."

"Record everything your grandfather says."

Ephraim nodded, then squatted on the floor by Joseph's side, pulling ink bottles from his sash and scattering them before him.

Though he could not see his sons, Jacob leaned forward intently and swept them with his eyes.

The strength his father showed amazed Joseph. He realized it was sheer will. Tenderly Joseph reached his arm around his father.

Jacob smiled thanks. "I would bless Reuben."

Seventy-year-old Reuben kneeled by his father's bed. Joseph guided his father's hands to Reuben's head.

"Reuben, you are my firstborn, my might, the beginning of my strength, with excellency of dignity, and excellency of power." Tears squeezed from his eyes. His voice husky, he continued, "But you have been unstable as water. You shall not excel. Because you defiled my bed, the blessing is removed from you." Reuben stumbled to his feet, tears smudged in his beard. Joseph looked at his oldest brother with compassion. Reuben's blessing had been more curse than blessing.

The twins, Simeon and Levi, knelt next. Jacob frowned as he laid his hands on their heads. "Simeon and Levi, you dishonored my name by your cruelties and wanton murder at Shechem. Cursed be you because of your anger. You shall be divided in your blessings and scattered in Israel."

Judah knelt. Jacob paused and looked toward heaven. "Judah, you are the one your brothers should praise. Your hand shall be in the neck of your enemies. Your father's children shall bow before you. The scepter shall not depart from Judah, nor a lawgiver from between his feet, until Shiloh come; and unto him shall the gathering of the people be."

Chills went up Joseph's spine. What his father had just said was that the promised Redeemer would come through Judah's lineage.

Each of Israel's sons: Zebulon, Issachar, Dan, Gad, Asher, and Napthali knelt before Jacob to receive his specific blessing. Joseph and Benjamin turn came last. Joseph knelt, knees cushioned on the rugs. He felt his father's frail trembling hands. He listened.

"Joseph is a fruitful bough, even a fruitful bough by a well, whose branches run over the wall. The blessings of your father have prevailed above the blessings of my progenitors unto the utmost bound of the everlasting hills; they shall be on the head of Joseph, and on the crown of the head of him that was separated from his brethren." He motioned. An old servant brought a tattered, stained and faded rag and placed it in Jacob's hands. Brothers craned to see. Whispers moved quickly through the brothers. "It is the coat of many colors. Joseph's coat."

Jacob held the cloth reverently. He fondled it as if he saw it. His hands on the rag, he gazed around the room with sightless eyes. "Even as this remnant of my son's coat has been preserved," he said solemnly, "so shall a remnant of the seed of my son be preserved by the hand of God, while the remainder of the seed of Joseph shall perish, even as the remnant of this garment."

Only Benjamin's blessing remained. He knelt before his father. Jacob spoke tenderly to his youngest, then lay back tiredly. He spoke weakly, "Now I can die and be gathered unto my people. Carry me up from Egypt and bury me in the cave of Machpelach as I have commanded you." His voice faded as he gave assignments for carrying his bier. His sons gathered close to hear him.

Judah stepped close and said, "Father, all you have commanded us, so we will do."

"God will be with you when you keep all his ways," Jacob sighed. "Turn not from his ways." He paused to get his breath. "Many troubles will befall you in the latter days in this land, but if your children and your children's children serve the Lord, He will save you from all trouble." Moments passed. "If you serve God and teach your children after you to know the Lord, then will the Lord raise up unto you and your children a servant from amongst your children. The Lord will deliver you and bring you out of Egypt and bring you back to the land of your fathers to inherit it."

Jacob sagged on his pillows. Joseph, sitting close, leaned over. Jacob's eyes were shut. He watched his father's breathing slow, then stop. Jacob, whom the Lord named Israel, had died.

Joseph turned Jacob's body over to the Egyptian embalmers. Forty days they worked on it. With embalming complete, Pharaoh declared seventy days of mourning throughout the land. Joseph journeyed to the palace to see Pharaoh. When he was announced, Pharaoh sat alone, waiting. It surprised Joseph to see how Amenhotep had aged. Then he smiled. He, himself, had just passed his fifty-sixth birthday. Amenhotep stepped from the dais, and the two friends embraced. Joseph had not been to the palace for several months, and he knew Amenhotep, though surrounded by nobles and advisors, was lonely. As they walked to the garden, Pharaoh said, "For seventy days our people have mourned the death of your father."

"Yes, my king. My family appreciates your declaration of a period of state mourning. One more favor I need ask."

Amenhotep raised his eyebrows.

"For twenty-seven years I have served you faithfully. Never have I asked anything for myself."

"True."

"My king, if I have found favor in your sight, then I must ask a personal favor."

"Whatever you ask, my friend: my treasure, more land, another wife?" Joseph smiled. "No, my king. Before my father died, I promised I would return his body to his land — the land of Canaan — for burial with his family. I ask you to grant me time to go with my father's body. After his funeral and burial I shall return."

"By all means, Joseph. Go up to Canaan. I shall send with you a funeral cortege which will never again be matched in the land of Canaan."

Pharaoh was as good as his word. Not only were Joseph's brothers and their older children in the procession, but all the nobles and advisors of the Pharaoh. Hyksos held the territory of Canaan, and Amenhotep put on a show of strength for the local people. One hundred fine chariots, each with a matched team, a driver and a bowman, led the funeral procession. Nobles, elders, and mourners rode in fine carriages, both before and after the carriage which carried the casket of Jacob. Immediately behind the mourners rode one hundred mounted warriors.

They traveled up the coast, through the land of the Philistines. They turned inland at the port of Jamnia, traveling the breadth of the land of Canaan, through the Canaanite cities of Eltekeh, Beth-horon, Gibeon, Bethel, and Jericho. Canaanites lined the roads. They had never seen such a procession. Armed and mounted warriors, chariots, wagons loaded with finely-dressed nobles, flags and banners, preceded and followed the funeral carriage. Runners ran ahead to the next towns to tell of the approaching cortege.

Joseph, following Pharaoh's instructions, did not stop the procession at the Jordan, but crossed over to the plains of Moab. They pitched tents around the small Moabite town of Atad. There Joseph and his people mourned Jacob for seven days. Following the funeral at Atad, they struck their tents and ponderously moved back across the Jordan. Joseph led the procession back through Jericho, then up the trail to Moriah. From Moriah they descended through the valley of Hebron until they camped before the tomb of Machpelach.

The sons, and Ephraim and Manasseh, lined up around the bier as Jacob had commanded. In solemn procession, they carried Jacob's casket on their shoulders into the dim recesses of the cave. Joseph went before, holding torch high. He pushed his way through cobwebs and decades of dust. Footsteps of his brothers and sons were the only sounds as they entered a room deep in the cave. There lay five stone caskets, dusty with age.

Joseph brushed dust away to read the inscriptions: "Abraham,... Sarah,... Isaac,... Rebecca," he read aloud. "This is a hallowed spot." A newer casket bore the inscription of Leah. "This is where the body of Father will lie," he said. "Near his dear wife, Leah." Reuben, who had been solemn-faced since Jacob's blessing, smiled at the thought of Jacob lying beside his mother.

The sarcophagus of Jacob settled down into the deep dust. Jacob was home. Joseph had fulfilled his promise.

Chapter 22: Death of Joseph

Joseph's eyes, though rheumy, twinkled as he talked. Servants propped him up on his bed in the great hall of his estate. Here he had chosen to die — a room of many memories. Here he had married Asenath before Pharaoh. Here he had seen his brothers when they made their first journey to Egypt. Here he had revealed to them his real identity. Though blue paint dimmed and peeled with age, for Joseph the room had special warmth.

His daughter, Rebecca, sat on the edge of the bed. Rachel and Osnath had both made short visits, then returned to their children. At the foot of the bed knelt his sons, Ephraim and Manasseh. Manasseh's once black hair was now as white as his father's. Ephraim, fair-haired as a youth, was as bald as the game pieces on the senet board. The contrast did not end there. Manasseh was tall, gangly, and thin; Ephraim, stout and well-rounded.

A commotion outside the door drew Joseph's eyes. The door opened to reveal his brothers. He raised his hand in a weary greeting, then smiled to himself. He was next to the youngest, yet he was the second to die. Only Benjamin preceded him in death.

But he had no regrets. He had lived a full and wonderful life. The Lord had truly blessed him. It would be good to meet the One God face to face. And Asenath? She had been gone now for over ten years. Oh, to see her sweet face again, and to feel her in his arms.

The ten old and stooped brothers stood around Joseph's bed. Lines of care filled their faces as maps show lines of streams and mountains. They had come to pay respect to Joseph who had become ruler of them all. All ten came forward to the bed, some whispering words of sorrow, others touching him to show their compassion. Joseph's arms felt as if they were made of bronze. He signaled a greeting to his family with his eyes.

Joseph turned his ancient head and gazed out the window at his blooming orchards. Soon the Nile would flood, signaling another new year. For ten years Joseph had lived alone with his thoughts. Asenath, Benjamin, Amunebet, Desir, Amenhotep . . . all had died. Death would be a relief for him. For eighty years he had governed Egypt. As his prophetic eyes saw the future, he had been saddened as well as thrilled. He wanted to shout praises to Jehovah.

Judah said aloud, "You look well, my brother."

Joseph, his voice weak and raspy, said, "Judah, my brother, it is too late for falsehoods." He lifted his thin shoulders, then let them fall. "For ninety-three years I have lived in his land." He paused to reflect, then continued, his voice breaking as he told them of things to come — things he had seen would befall their people. The brothers seemed shocked at his words. They listened in silence as he related to them Israel's future as slaves to the Egyptians. A murmuring arose from his brothers.

"Do not despair," he said. "I have seen in vision that God will visit our descendants and bring them out of Egypt to the land of promise." He paused for breath, then continued. "My brothers, promise me when the time comes that God takes our people back to the promised land, you will have them take my bones, that I might also be buried in the land of my fathers."

"So be it," Judah said. The other brothers chorused their affirmations.

Machir, Manasseh's oldest son, left the throng of people and came to stand beside his father. Joseph winked at his grandson. His mind wandered. How swiftly time had passed. Machir's daughter, Newfru, his great-granddaughter, was almost twenty years of age. Joseph had given up trying to count his many descendants. With the marriage of Ephraim's grandson, Seth, to Anat-her, the granddaughter of Benjamin, Joseph had seen three generations of Ephraim's children.

His eyes opened. His brothers and their children still stood by the bed. He breathed deeply and sighed, "I die, and go unto my fathers." He smiled. "But I go down to my grave with joy."

He was suddenly tired and shut his eyes. Faintly, as if at a distance, he heard Manasseh trying to usher out the rest of the family. He opened his eyes. "Hold," he whispered hoarsely.

They stopped and turned to him. "Promise me once again that when Israel returns to the land of our fathers, that you will bring up my bones with you from here."

Judah said, "We so promise." Joseph nodded in satisfaction, closed his eyes, and laid his head back into the pillow.

It was nighttime when Joseph awakened. By light of a flickering candle, he looked at his sleeping children. He silently praised the Lord. What a strength his children had been through the years. When his eyes strayed back to Rebecca, he saw her eyes were open.

"Father," she whispered. "May I get you some hot gruel?"

He shook his head. "No, my daughter. But I do thirst."

Rebecca put a cup to his lips. He sipped some of the warm tea, then sank back, exhausted. One more task remained to be completed. "Please wake Ephraim," he asked. His voice was quieter now, and he did not want it to fail him.

When Ephraim stood next to the bed, Joseph asked, "Dear Son, the Lord has shown his revelations to me. The record must be completed." Ephraim nodded and gathered his writing tools and papyrus. He sat on the bed, close to Joseph's face, a board on his lap on which he had placed the papyrus.

"I have given you charge of the records," Joseph whispered. "When you complete the records, transcribe them onto the bronze plates. They must be passed on to your children so the record will be preserved to future generations."

"I shall see that it is done, Father."

"Good." Joseph's eyes took on a faraway look. It was as if he had already left the room. "Please write."

Ephraim sat, brush poised over the papyrus.

Joseph spoke, quietly and prophetically, "The Lord said, 'A seer will I raise up to deliver my people out of the land of Egypt. I will make him great in my eyes, for he shall do my work. After the prophet delivers my people out of Egypt in the days of their bondage, they shall be scattered again. Nevertheless, they shall be remembered in the covenants of the Lord, when the Messiah comes.'" Joseph continued speaking, naming the seer and telling of his great work among the children of Israel.

Manasseh had awakened. He leaned forward intently, anxious to hear his father's words. When it appeared that Joseph was through talking, he asked, "Father, what important message would you pass on to your children?"

For a few moments it appeared that Joseph had not heard, then he whispered, "I experienced a terrible empty feeling — a loneliness from being separated from those I loved. Comfort came when I remembered I could pray and be heard and helped. We can always be in touch with a powerful Friend who loves us and helps us, in His own time, and in His own way." He sighed. "I often did not understand how the One God directed my life. But the realization finally came that we can pray to our God and He will hear our prayers and help us in the way that is best for us." The last few words faded as Joseph fought for breath. Speaking had exhausted him. His head sagged on the pillow. His breath came in ragged and shallow gasps. Ephraim looked anxiously at his father. Rebecca bathed Joseph's head with a damp cloth.

Joseph roused himself. He sighed a great sigh and turned his head to look at Rebecca. He started to speak but his voice failed. Rebecca leaned down so her ear was by his mouth. Whispering, he said, "My dear child. Know I love you. I have now finished the work."

She again wiped the perspiration from his brow. He whispered something else. She bent low again to hear. "Keep the faith. Keep the faith." Joseph had spoken his last words.

Epilogue

The Egyptians embalmed Joseph in kingly fashion, as befitted a ruler of Egypt. True to their promise, the brothers refused to let him be buried. They placed his body in a coffin and hid the coffin. Ephraim wrote his father's epitaph, then inscribed onto the bronze plates the final words dealing with his father, Joseph of the Covenant Coat:

"*So Joseph died when he was an hundred and ten years old; and they embalmed him, and they put him in a coffin in Egypt; and he was kept from burial by the children of Israel, that he might be carried up and laid in the sepulchre with his father. And thus they remembered the oath which they sware unto him.*"

Pharaoh, after Joseph's death, did not treat the children of Israel with compassion. He built a new palace in Avaris, conscripting a work force from the children of Israel.

Ephraim, true to the promise he made his father, faithfully kept the record of the people. He used as the beginning date of his chronology the date when Jacob and his family came down to Egypt from Hebron. He wrote of the passing of his remaining ten uncles, the sons of Jacob. The year after Joseph's death, the seventy-second year after Jacob had come down to Egypt, Zebulon died at one hundred and fourteen. Three years later, the warrior Simeon died at one hundred and twenty. In the seventy-ninth year the oldest brother, Reuben died at one hundred and twenty-five. For several years a brother died each year. Dan, in the eightieth year, at one hundred and twenty; Issachar, the next year, at one hundred and twenty-two; the next year Asher died at one hundred and twenty-three; and then the following year, the eighty-third year, Gad died, one hundred and twenty-five.

Judah died at one hundred twenty-nine during the eighty-sixth year, and Napthali, at one hundred thirty-two, died in the eighty-ninth year. The sole survivor, Levi, he whose descendants would be the priests of the children of Israel, died in the ninety-third year after Jacob and his family came to Egypt. He was one hundred and thirty-seven. The sons of Jacob were no more on the earth, but their numerous descendants became a real concern to Pharaoh. His advisors continually asked, "What do we do with this growing and powerful tribe?" In the one hundred and second year of Israel's going down to Egypt, Pharaoh died and Melol, his son, reigned in his stead. He was a Pharaoh who knew not Joseph.

Ephraim wrote, "Now there arose a new king over Egypt, which knew not Joseph. And he said unto his people, Behold, the people of the children of Israel are more and mightier than we. Come, let us deal wisely with them lest they multiply and fight against us." The children of Israel went to bed one night a free people, guests of the sovereign of Egypt. They awoke the next morning slaves, their towns and villages surrounded by Pharaoh's chariots. Even as slaves they continued to multiply.

The one hundred and thirty-fifth year saw several of Joseph's prophecies fulfilled. A child was born of the tribe of Levi. The Egyptians, attempting to stop the burgeoning population of the Israelites, decreed that all male children would die. To prevent this baby's death, his mother placed him in a basket and floated him to the palace. Pharaoh's daughter drew him out of the water and raised him as royalty. She named him Moses.

When he was eighty years old, two hundred and fifteen years from the time Jacob went down to Egypt, Moses led the children of Israel out of Egypt to the Promised Land. For forty years they wandered, carrying the body of Joseph. Everywhere they wandered, he went with them. After finally crossing the Jordan into the Promised Land under direction of Joshua, Joseph was buried — not with his father and forebears at Machpelach — but in the plot of ground that Jacob had bought near Shechem. Joseph had come home.

Joseph was dead, but his prophecies were for all people of all times. He of the covenant coat had fulfilled his promise. By being a servant to all, he became a ruler of many. By serving others, his name is inscribed forever in the Lamb's Book of Life.

Preview of Coming Attractions

I, Nephi, book two of the Nephite Chronicles, will be available in December 2006, just in time for Christmas purchasing.

Nephi was engraver of golden plates, prophet of ancient America, son, father, whose nation was destined to perish by the sword of the people of his brothers, Laman and Lemuel.

But what about the childhood of Nephi? What about his journey in the wilderness with his father? What gave this mighty man of God the strength he needed to build a ship under the Lord's guidance and to control the constant anger and threatenings of his rebellious brothers?

Experience gained when Nephi was but a lad is told in colorful detail as he travels in the desert caravan with his merchant father, Lehi. The family leaves Jerusalem after Lehi is told, in a vision, that the city will soon be destroyed. Nephi returns with his brothers for the brass plates, held by Laban. Deserted by his faith-hearted brothers, Nephi, at the Lord's command, kills Laban. Thus Lehi gains possession of the genealogy of his fathers. He marries one of the daughters of Ishmael, and starts his family while in the desert. For years the family of Lehi wanders in the desert as nomad tent-dwellers. During these years, events that help Nephi become mighty in stature, physically and spiritually, are given the sheen of reality.

How Nephi is able to build a ship capable of sailing the great waters of Irreantum is related. The terrible storm that strikes and almost sinks the ship after his mutinous brothers tie Nephi to the mast is rousing drama.

The story follows Lehi and his family after they reach the Land of Promise. Nephi continues to commune with the Lord, but he finally abandons his long-suffering efforts to turn his brothers from their wicked ways. After he narrowly escapes death at their hands, he takes his family and followers far inland in what is, for Nephi, a final journey.

I, Nephi is warm, colorful believable fiction. The reader will be caught and held as the life of this remarkable man of God involves and changes the lives of those around him. This book is sure to become a classic in Mormon Literature.

The Nephite Chronicles Series by Robert H. Moss

Covenant Coat: *A Novel of Joseph*—Sold as a slave by his brothers, Joseph is carried into Egypt and spends many years as a slave or in prison before God makes him an instrument of salvation. But Joseph readily forgives his brothers and repays treachery with love. He changes—from taking to giving, from dependence to independence, from arrogance to humility. This is the dramatic re-telling of a great Biblical epic.

I, Nephi: *A Novel of Nephi*—This intriguing fictional account sweeps the reader back to the time of this great Book of Mormon prophet. In colorful detail it follows his life as a boy in the desert; the struggle with his rebellious brothers, Laman and Lemuel; his sojourn in the promised land; and his relationship with God as a prophet and leader of his people. This insightful book captures the romance, rebellion, prophecy and adventure of an era when warring factions divided into two great nations.

The Waters of Mormon: *A Novel of Alma the Elder*—More than just another Book of Mormon story, The Waters of Mormon is an intriguing adventure. It's a moving story of repentance, a powerful tale of love between husband and wife and parent and child. Most certainly it is a father and son story as it focuses on the two Alma's and their relationship. It will touch your heart and leave you with profound insights concerning these people, their times, and the Gospel principles which shaped their lives.

That I Were an Angel: *A Novel of Alma the Younger*—Why did Alma, the Younger, rebel against his father and against the Church? What was his process of repentance? How did Alma, as a parent, handle a rebellious son? Why the Angel? That I Were An Angel gives intriguing answers to these questions in Alma's own words. This is his history, told by himself, shedding light on rebellious youth in all ages of time.

Title of Liberty: *A Novel of Captain Moroni and Helaman*—Moroni and Helaman were men with a cause: preserving the liberty and religion of the Nephite people. Moroni, a professional warrior and commander of the Nephite armies, fought throughout his life for the cause of liberty. He raised the Title of Liberty for the Nephite people, inspiring them to action. Helaman, trained as a scribe and serving as the High Priest, was an unlikely candidate for an army commander, but with God's help he accomplished what few other commanders could have with his 2000 Ammonite youth.

The Abridger: *A Novel of Mormon*—It was Mormon's calling to abridge hundreds of plates—the total records of the Nephite people—into the Book of Mormon as it is found at present. Through his goal setting and accomplishment of those goals, we have the Book of Mormon as sacred scripture for our day. Mormon was a powerful man, both in body and spirit. Chosen to lead the Nephite armies while still but a youth, he fulfilled that responsibility for sixty years. Then, as an old man, he completed his most important role: that of scribe and abridger.

Valiant Witness: *A Novel of Moroni*—This warm fictional account charts the life of Moroni. Of special interest are the lonely years between the final Nephite battle and the end of his writings. It describes his courage as a young warrior and details his love and marriage, his wide-ranging travels and his ministry as one of the Lord's disciples. It gives insight into his personal joys and sorrows and his sojourn in the spirit world. Fourteen hundred years after his death, we see his commitment and determination as the restorer of the Gospel to the earth through the Prophet Joseph Smith. This book will help you know this great man like never before.

Capstone of Faith—This final book of the Nephite Chronicles series, instead of focusing on a particular hero in the Book of Mormon, focuses on a person—a person just like you and me—who through right choices, develops hero characteristics; not necessarily those that make a person a hero in battle, but those traits of moral courage, forgiveness, honesty, and integrity that win the battles of daily living. This book is not the typical boy meets girl, they fall in love and get married type of love story. The real emphasis is looking at a person who seeks truth and finds it.